POWER REGIMES

Mapping The DNA Of Business And Supply Chain Relationships

Andrew Cox
Joe Sanderson
Glyn Watson

Earlsgate Press

Published by Earlsgate Press.
(www.earlsgatepress.com)

© Andrew Cox, Joe Sanderson and Glyn Watson 2000

First published: May 2000

All rights reserved. No part of this publication may be reproduced, stored in a retrieval system or transmitted in any form or by any means, electronic, mechanical, photocopying, recorded or otherwise, without the prior permission of the publisher.

British Library Cataloguing in Publication Data

A catalogue record of this book is available from the British Library.

ISBN 1-873439-91-1

Printed in Great Britain by Bookcraft, Midsomer Norton, Somerset.

Contents

Preface: vii

1 Introduction   1

2 What Is Business Power?   11

3 Mapping The Attributes Of Power: The DNA Of Business Life   21

4 Blue Eyes And Brown Hair: Making Sense Of Supply Chain Individuality   37

5 Love And Marriage In Supply Chains   51

6 Making Choices And Learning To Live With Them   65

7 Re-engineering The DNA Of Business And Supply Chain Life   81

LIST OF FIGURES AND TABLES

Fig. 1	Potential Buyer-Supplier Business to Business Exchange Relationships	18
Fig. 2	The Relative Utility of Firm Resources	27
Fig. 3	Value Appropriation in Double-Dyad Exchange Regimes	41
Fig. 4	Value Appropriation in Complex Power Regimes	48
Fig. 5	Relationship Portfolio Analysis	56
Fig 6	Power and Relationship Management Matrix	61

| Table 1 | Mechanisms That Impede Imitative Competition | 30 |

ABOUT THE AUTHORS

Professor Andrew Cox is Director of the Centre for Business Strategy and Procurement (CBSP) at The University of Birmingham's Business School in the UK. He is also Chairman of Robertson Cox Ltd, a US and UK based competence development consultancy. (www.robertsoncox.com)

Dr Glyn Watson is Lecturer in Supply and Value Chain Management at the Centre for Business Strategy and Procurement (CBSP) at the University of Birmingham in the UK. He has written extensively on the subject of business and supply chain management and has also acted as a consultant to a number of organisations.

Dr Joe Sanderson is a Research Fellow at the Centre for Business Strategy and Procurement (CBSP) at the University of Birmingham in the UK. He has published in the area of both supply chain management and political economy. In 1997, he published *The Political Economy of Modern Britain*, in collaboration with Andrew Cox.

Other business related publications by the authors available from *Earlsgate Press* (at: www.earlsgatepress.com):

Effective Supply Chain Management
by Andrew Cox
ISBN 1-873439-96-2

The QV Way: Better Practice Methodologies for Effective Outsourcing and Supply Chain Management
by Andrew Cox
ISBN 1-873439-86-5

Outsourcing: A Business Guide to Risk Management Tools and Techniques
by Christopher Lonsdale and Andrew Cox
ISBN 1-873439-61-X

Strategic Procurement Management: Concepts and Cases
edited by Richard Lamming and Andrew Cox
ISBN 1-873439-81-4

Business Success: A Way of Thinking About Strategy, Critical Supply Chain Assets and Operational Best Practice
by Andrew Cox
ISBN 1-873439-76-8

Advanced Supply Chain Management: The Best Practice Debate
edited by Andrew Cox and Peter Hines
ISBN 1-873439-51-2

PREFACE

This is a short volume that introduces the concept of *power regimes*. The book has been written as a non-technical guide for practitioners and as a complement to a much more academically detailed study entitled *Supply Chains, Markets and Power: Mapping Buyer and Supplier Power Regimes*. The aim of this volume is to provide practitioners with an easy step by step guide to what is a very complex issue. This issue is nothing less than an understanding of the principles factors that cause success and failure in business life.

If it is possible to outline the principles that govern success and failure in business then it will be also be possible one day for social scientists to claim that they have uncovered the DNA of business life. While we make no such claim in this small volume we present the concept of *power regimes* as a contribution to the development of a better understanding of the causes of success and failure in business.

Before outlining how the concepts of *power regimes* contribute to an understanding of the DNA of business life, it is perhaps instructive to recount the story of how — through a series of non-linear steps — the DNA of human life was eventually discovered. It is in our view instructive because the story of DNA, and the way of thinking that led to its discovery, has parallels with the way in which we believe the DNA of business life will eventually be mapped. To understand how the code of human existence was mapped we must begin with a journey that started in the mid-nineteenth century.

In 1865, the Morovian monk and part-time scientist, Gregor Mendel, presented a paper to 40 members of the little known Brunn Natural Science Society. The subject of this paper was peas. Mendel finished his presentation, received some polite applause and the small assembly shifted their attention to other matters. The next year, the paper was selected for inclusion in the Society's journal, the *Transactions of the Brunn Natural History Society*, under the title, 'Experiments on Plant Hybridisation'. Once again, the work received scant attention. The following year, when he was promoted to Abbot of his monastery, he put his scientific studies to one side and devoted the remainder of his life to his clerical duties.

Apparently, Mendel felt no bitterness towards his fellow scientists. In fact, he remained confident his contribution to biology would be recognised one day. Indeed, he is reported to have commented to a friend that 'Meine Zeit wird schon Kommen' ('My time will come'). He was to be proved right, but not in his lifetime. Mendel died in 1884, unrecognised, his work overshadowed by Charles Darwin's *On the Origin of Species*. Since then, however, he has secured his place in history.

Mendel's great contribution to biological science was to suggest that whilst even within a species nature exhibited almost infinite variety, this individuality was not haphazard. Using a series of detailed experiments, he showed that an offspring ultimately owed its form to its parents. On one level, there was nothing particularly startling in this idea. For years, biologists had argued that children were a blend of their parents. However, the writers who had preceded Mendel had thought children to be some sort of biological average. So, if a child's father had a long pointy nose and its mother a short and snub one, then the child would have a nose of about average size. Mendel, however, showed that this was not the case and that, in fact, all offspring (of whatever species) inherited specific characteristics from a particular parent. A child may owe its nose to one parent, but could well owe its size and hair colour to the other.

His genius went beyond this simple proposition, however, as he demonstrated that one could probabilistically link biological output with input. Inheriting a particular characteristic from a particular parent, he argued, was not a random event. Rather, his experiments showed that when he cross-fertilised pure strains of plant, the next generation was three times more likely to exhibit the characteristics of one of the parents than they were the other. That is, his second-generation peas were three times more likely to be round than wrinkled and three times more likely to be yellow than green.

Mendel conjectured that while an individual organism inherited the characteristics (genes) of both parents, some genetic types were dominant whilst others were recessive. Today, the two alternative types of gene are referred to as alleles. If during the process of reproduction, two dominant alleles come into contact, then there is little question of what will result. If yellow is the dominant characteristic of a pea, whilst green is the recessive one, then a second-generation pea taking the yellow allele from each parent will itself be yellow. If it takes a yellow from one of the parents and a green from the other, it will still be yellow. Only if the offspring inherits two recessive genes will it be the proverbial pea green.

As with even the greatest discoveries, there were gaps in Mendel's thinking, not least of which was the inability to explain the mechanism through which inheritance was communicated down through the generations. This problem was a difficult one, which took years and the efforts of many scientists to uncover. The puzzle was finally solved by two Cambridge academics, British physicist Francis Crick and American biologist James Watson. They showed that the root of an organism's individuality lies in its chemical make-up, something that resides in a double-stranded molecule.

This molecule glorifies in the technical name of deoxyribonucleic acid, better known to the rest of us as DNA. Each strand consists of phosphates, sugars and bases. These bases act like the rungs of a ladder, joining each strand together. It is these bases and base combinations that literally tell the body how to build itself and precisely what form to take.

But what, the reader asks, has this history lesson in biology to do with an understanding of the causes of success and failure in business life? The answer is that in business money can only be made successfully by the creation of supply chains that deliver highly valued products and services to final consumers. To be successful, however, the individuals and/or companies that participate in the supply chains (or complex networks of buyer and seller supply relationships) must be able to earn a sustainable financial return from owning and/or controlling particular resources in any chain.

PREFACE

Although it may not at first be self-evident, the supply chains that we have just described are actually a bit like human organisms. Every supply chain is unique, just as every human being is unique. No two chains or human beings are alike. Descriptively this should be obvious. The effort and requirement that go into making an aeroplane are clearly different to that which go into producing a new drug, a building or offering someone a legal service.

This uniqueness is not simply descriptive, it is also analytical. It is not simply a matter of different people, performing different tasks to produce different products and services. Rather, the analytical properties that underpin the exchange process in every supply chain are also different. This impacts directly on the ability of anyone to manage a chain, and indeed, the techniques that should be employed when doing so.

Individual and unique does not, however, mean random. Amid all of the complexity, it is possible to determine patterns and regularities that allow the manager to make sense of his or her universe. The concept that allows the supply chain manager to put together the supply chain jigsaw is *power*.

Power and its meaning are much discussed elsewhere, but it is used here to indicate the ability of one actor to adversely affect the interests of another. Every firm that interacts with customers and suppliers is involved in sets of power relationships. The firm's capacity to make money depends on its ability to manage these relationships to its advantage. No firm that finds itself sandwiched between powerful sets of customers and suppliers will be able to make sustainable and high returns. Conversely, firms that manage to take effective control of (have power in) their commercial environment tend to make a great deal of money.

In the real world, of course, a firm is likely to find that it has power over some customers and suppliers but not others. Sometimes it is the other party that will have power, sometimes there will be a balance of power. In fact in buyer-supplier business relationships there are four basic types of power relation: *buyer dominance*, *supplier dominance*, *buyer-supplier interdependence* and *buyer-supplier independence*. Within the DNA analogy, these supply chain relationship power types equate to the genetic traits of an organism. Whilst the reasons why particular power relations arise in particular circumstances vary (a subject that forms part of the story of this volume), all supply chain exchange relationships fall into one of these four basic categories.

What is just as interesting as these structures of power are the supply chain resources that cause them to arise in the first instance. For products or services to be provided to final customers, a supply chain has to bring together a whole array of resources (both tangible and intangible). These resources are owned either by buyers or by suppliers in the chain, and it is these resources or, rather, resource combinations, that are the DNA of business life.

Consequently, supply chains can be conceived of as vast networks of dyadic (buyer and seller) power relationships. Taken as a whole, the supply chain that must be created to deliver any product or service can be conceived of as a particular *power regime*. The overall structure of each regime depends on the unique power relationships between buyers and sellers in all of its constituent parts. This is why we argue that it is likely that every supply chain will tend to be unique, even though – like human beings – each supply chain is made up of the same generic power structures (just as in the case of human beings we are all unique, but we are also made up of the same bases, sugars and phosphates).

Of course, *power regimes*, unlike biological organisms, are not static. If a pea is born green it cannot hope to turn itself yellow. By the same token, none of the authors is likely, overnight (or indeed in a month of Sundays) to turn themselves into a world class sprinter. If a biological organism fails to manifest a useful trait or skill it must be hoped that its offspring will be luckier, although by Mendel's reckoning luck has very little to do with it. This is one reason why it is important that the DNA metaphor not be taken too far.

Supply chains can be (and routinely are) genetically re-engineered. Sometimes this is as a consequence of a firm's deliberate attempts to reconfigure a *power regime* to improve its place within it, or to make the task of management easier. On other occasions, a firm may be an unintended beneficiary or victim of the actions of others. However, in order to take some of the luck out of the game it is useful if it is possible for practitioners to at least understand the rules of the supply chain management game. Hence the reason for this volume.

In writing this volume we owe a significant debt of gratitude to a large number of parties. Firstly, thanks are owed to the Engineering and Physical Sciences Research Council for financially supporting our research (Project No. GR/L86395). Thanks must also go to the numerous writers and commentators who have helped to shape the thinking herein. Some of these authors are cited within these pages, but regrettably we have been unable to include all of those to whom we owe a debt of gratitude over the many years of our research.

Finally, there are the personal expressions of thanks. Professionally, these go to Paul Ireland, Chris Lonsdale and Andy Passey for their assistance on the larger academic volume and to Jackie Potter and Michele Donovan for their administrative support. Universities could not function without this administrative assistance and there are those (the current authors among them) who believe that the administrative staff often make a greater contribution than the academics. On a social level, the authors would like to express their gratitude to their families. The first and major casualties of any academic undertaking are the people who provide the authors with the greatest support. So, it is to our respective families (or kinship support networks to use the modern jargon) that this book is dedicated.

ANDREW COX
JOE SANDERSON
GLYN WATSON

CENTRE FOR BUSINESS STRATEGY AND PROCUREMENT
UNIVERSITY OF BIRMINGHAM
APRIL 2000

CHAPTER 1

INTRODUCTION

Although the title of this book is *Power Regimes*, this short book is actually about supply chains and supply chain types. There has been a great deal written about supply chains in recent years, but comparatively little on supply chain types. This is no accident and the two things are not entirely unrelated. It is the nature of what has been written about supply chains to date that has played a major role in limiting enquiry into the issue of diversity.

Every year, there is a new hot topic or fad that occupies the pages of business management journals. In recent years, EVA, BPR and core competence thinking have all been prominent. If they are lucky (or rather, if the ideas prove to be of demonstrable value), these business fads will have an extended run. Currently, it appears that the concept of integrated supply chain management is pre-eminent, and indeed it is now commonplace for supply chain management to be discussed, by academics and practitioners alike, as a key element in the pursuit by firms of competitive advantage.

2   POWER REGIMES

The enhanced profile of supply chain thinking within many companies can largely be explained by the phenomenal success of Japanese industry, particularly in the automotive sector in the late 1970s and early 1980s. Western business leaders and academics at that time were quite rightly concerned to understand why American and European firms were haemorrhaging market share to their Japanese competitors. This concern led to a team of British and American academics undertaking what was effectively a massive benchmarking exercise into the phenomenon.

The main conclusion derived from this research by Womack, Jones and Roos, the three researchers concerned, was that the secret of Japanese business success lay largely in a preference for open, collaborative and long-term relationships (or 'partnerships') with suppliers in a co-ordinated supply chain. This way of working was contrasted starkly with the Western penchant for short-term, arm's-length supply relationships established through adversarial, open market competition. The use of collaborative and co-ordinated supply relationships, it was argued, was a crucial means by which Japanese companies were able to enhance their operational efficiency and effectiveness and, thereby, maintain a competitive edge. This idea is at the heart of what has more recently been called the 'lean enterprise'.

The lean enterprise approach to supply chain management is now firmly established as the dominant paradigm in most of the literature about procurement and supply. A survey of the work of commentators like Christopher, Harrison, Hines, Lamming, Macbeth and Ferguson, Saunders, and Gattorna and Walters confirms this. Indeed, the notion that collaboration delivers greater business benefits than competition has also become commonplace in the broader strategic management writing as well. Companies are being told that strategic alliances with their erstwhile competitors are becoming an imperative rather than an option in many industries. Some writers on business strategy have gone so far as to argue either that competition is dead (as Moore has done), or that 'co-opetition' rather than competition is the secret of success (the position taken by Brandenburger and Nalebuff).

The fundamental premise of the lean enterprise approach is that competitive advantage will be derived from collaboration or 'partnership' throughout the supply chain in order to reduce various forms of waste and, thereby, deliver exceptional value to the end customer. Furthermore, everyone taking part in the exercise should benefit. Part of being in a partnership means sharing and this means allocating the pains and gains of the association on a more or less equal basis.

However, despite the widespread acceptance of these ideas the lean enterprise model has recently begun to attract an increasing amount of criticism. Many firms have found that partnerships with their suppliers have failed to deliver the expected benefits in terms of cost reduction, quality improvement or innovation. Even when such benefits have been achieved, firms have discovered that not everyone has benefited (or at least benefited equally) from their association with the other supply chain members.

If it was lean supply, it was lean supply of the *oneeyed* variety. That is to say, there have been efficiency savings, but without the sharing of benefits amongst all participants. These apparent failures have led two writers, Kapoor and Gupta, to go as far as to suggest that there should be a return to 'aggressive sourcing' based on free-market principles rather than collaboration. The criticisms levelled against the lean approach can be placed into two broad categories: the 'problem of competitive imitation' and the 'problem of appropriateness'.

The authors have discussed the problem of competitive imitation elsewhere. In essence, this work echoes Michael Porter's 1996 observation that a sustainable competitive advantage cannot be built upon easily imitated tools and techniques designed solely to enhance a firm's operational efficiency. The problem is that improvements in operational efficiency, while pushing back the productivity frontier, will inevitably encourage imitation. If, like the lean enterprise model, the basis of these efficiency improvements is clearly and explicitly documented, then it will quickly be diffused and the general level of efficiency will be commensurately enhanced. It follows that absolute improvement for everyone means relative improvement for no one.

While this is undoubtedly a serious criticism, our concern in this volume is with the second difficulty sometimes associated with lean thinking, the problem of appropriateness. Because of the prevalence of lean supply thinking amongst practitioners, until relatively recently few observers gave much thought to the idea of supply chain types and whether or not it was appropriate to use particular supply management strategies under specific supply chain circumstances.

Since the champions of lean believe the idea has almost universal applicability in all supply chain circumstances it has never occurred to them that what they are advocating may not be appropriate in some supply chain circumstances. Even those who do not think this way have tended to believe however that the principles of lean have widespread relevance in most supply chain circumstances. Logically, therefore, it made little sense for commentators or practitioners to ask the question – do supply chains differ? – because the answer was of little significance. It made more sense to dedicate effort towards finding ways to make the new orthodoxy work rather than question whether it is appropriate in all circumstances.

The problem with this approach has been twofold. First, it has been of little benefit for those practitioners for whom lean thinking is not appropriate. If lean techniques do not work for them, what tools and techniques should they to use in their place? Second, it has started to become clear that there are very many circumstances under which the ideas of collaborative partnership and integrated supply chain management are difficult to apply. The construction industry, for one, has very many supply chains in which lean ideas simply cannot be made to work.

Knowing that lean supply thinking does work in some circumstances but does not in others is helpful, but only up to a point. Practitioners are much more interested in understanding whether or not it is likely to work (or not) in their own specific cases, rather than knowing that it may or may not work in general. In order to be able to provide a guide to when lean thinking will and will not work, it becomes imperative that we understand not what lean thinking is, but rather under what circumstances lean thinking is appropriate.

To be able to understand this some form of classification of supply chain types must be undertaken. This is because we need to know which types of supply chains are conducive to lean approaches and which are not. For those that are not, alternative approaches will need to be developed.

Most recent attempts to codify supply chains have tended to be descriptive. That is, they have tended to organise supply chains on the basis of their physical characteristics. So, supply chains are divided on the basis of whether they are product or service, project or process, primary or secondary, and static or innovative. While heuristically useful, the benefits of this line of enquiry are analytically limited.

Firstly, very few supply chains can be neatly placed in such descriptive boxes. If we consider the IT supply chain it is clear that certain parts of it are project-based. The systems integration role, for example, might be described in this way. However, not all elements of a system integration supply chain would happily fit this label. For the PC manufacturer, whose machines are offered as part of the system integrator's package, the supply chain is more process-based than it is project. Similarly, in construction, the turnkey contractor may view the work as bespoke, but for the company supplying the bricks and mortar for the project it will clearly be routine business.

Similarly, supply chains do not readily conform to the simple dichotomy of static and innovative. Parts of a supply chain that exhibit rapid technological innovations sit alongside others that are technologically moribund. More important, perhaps, is the profound problem that few of the attempts at descriptive codification that have so far been undertaken have offered a systematic explanation for what the taxonomy or system of classification means in relation to the ways in which these different types should be managed.

The central idea presented within this volume is that the differences between supply chains are highly significant from an appropriateness of management point of view. Yet at the same time we do not subscribe to the notion that there are distinct supply chain types – at least in the conventional sense of the term. Supply chains are just too disparate, with so many unique properties, for us to be able to understand them on the basis of the simple descriptive classifications used by commentators thus far.

This does not mean, however, that all attempts at understanding the properties of supply chains are futile. As with biology, the processes that lead to supply chain individualism or uniqueness may be complex but they are not random. Supply chains have embedded in their structures certain sets of rules. These rules are explicable and capable of analytical classification. The basic unit of analysis for all supply chains is the dyadic power relationship between specific buyers and suppliers. Like the traits in an organism, taken together, these power relationships give the supply chain its shape. What, analytically, provides the unique structure in all supply chains are the multiple combinations of power relationships between buyers and suppliers throughout the chain.

Whilst, when looked at as a whole, supply chain structures are highly complicated, individual buyer-supplier relationships are not random. They can, in fact, only ever fall into one of four types. These types differ in relation to the structure of power that is created between the buyer and supplier in a dyadic exchange relationship. The four types of relationship that a buyer and supplier might experience are:

8 POWER REGIMES

- *Buyer Dominance*
- *Supplier Dominance*
- *Buyer-Supplier Interdependence*
- *Buyer-Supplier Independence*

Knowing this fact allows us to start to think about how particular buyer-supplier exchanges might fit together in an extended supply chain of business relationships. In this volume, we refer to this overall supply chain picture (or if you prefer jigsaw puzzle) as a *power regime*. By understanding the structure of power in any supply chain in this way it becomes possible to predict which players in the chain will be more or less likely to achieve business success or failure. Relatedly, it is also possible to predict which types of relationship management strategy are most likely to be successful under particular power regime circumstances.

We believe that this is the type of understanding that practitioners need. They do not need fads that lead to failure; what they really need is a way of thinking that allows them to understand the power regimes they are involved in and the most appropriate ways of managing in them to achieve sustainable business success. They need, therefore, nothing short of a guide to the DNA of business and supply chain life. We believe that if practitioners read carefully what is presented in this short volume they will be provided with many of the major signposts on that road.

The volume has the following structure. In chapter two, we provide a formal definition of power in buyer-supplier business relationships. In chapter three, we look at the key attributes of buyer and supplier power. This is the DNA of business and supply chain life. The resources that buyers and suppliers bring to an exchange determine which of the four basic power categories the relationship falls into.

Having mapped this code of business and supply chain life, in chapter four, we look at how the power-DNA categories combine to provide the big picture. Here, we look at power dynamics from a moneymaking perspective. Which parties stand to make most from a supply chain relationship and why? In chapter five, we turn to the issue of effective supply chain management. We discuss appropriateness in the choice of relationship management approaches by buyers and suppliers in the context of the four power positions. Four illustrative case studies in appropriateness are presented in this section. The final chapter draws some general conclusions about the utility of the model that we have presented, and addresses how practitioners may begin to utilise it for genuine business benefit.

CHAPTER II

WHAT IS BUSINESS POWER?

Power is a feature of everyday life. We use the term all of the time. It underpins many of our most important social relations. Many people feel uncomfortable with this assertion. After all, power has so many negative associations. It conjures up images of rifle butts, of secret plotting. In the movies, good guys wear white hats and try to help out the weak. The bad guys, on the other hand, dress in black and want to control people or appropriate things. Clearly, power is about these things, but it is not only about them. Its exercise is not always as obvious or its effects so sinister. Quite frequently, it shows itself in the most mundane of ways.

For example, when a boy meets a girl and they fall in love it does not end the power play between the sexes. Disputes will continue to arise over who should wash the car, walk the dog or clean the dishes. Who wins these little battles is likely to depend on the respective resources of the participants and the skill with which they deploy them. If there is a rough balance of power in the relationship then the distribution of responsibility will be determined by the old-fashioned principle of give-and-take. If one particular party has the power, however, then they may well choose to shirk on the housekeeping. Throughout the lifetime of the relationship, the balance of power is likely to shift between the two parties. But if one party should ever fall out of love then the other is likely to find him or herself at a grave disadvantage. Many marriages are emotionally abusive, even if they are not physically so.

Power is also important in other areas. It is central to an understanding of politics, for example. Differences of opinion over the way economies should be organised divided the continent of Europe for fifty years. One side saw market economics, with its emphasis on free will and individual freedom, as the best way of organising the processes of production and social (re)distribution. The other side held that Western freedoms were largely illusory and masked a class war that left the vast majority of people greatly disadvantaged. At root, what divided the two protagonists was a dispute over the structures of power in a capitalist society.

However, whilst power clearly plays a central part in helping to structure everyday life, what exactly is it? More importantly, what does it mean in a business and supply chain context?

Power, Gallie argued in 1955, is an 'essentially contested concept'. What he was implying was that it is a concept, the meaning of which cannot be formally verified, although it is amenable to rational debate. These difficulties can, of course, be overcome by using a working definition, which applies solely in the context of a specific study. The working definition of power that will be employed in this book is *the ability of one actor to affect the behaviour of another actor in a manner contrary to the second actor's interests.* This was the definition developed by Steven Lukes in his now classic study on the subject. It is not enough, however, to simply choose one definition from amongst the many on offer, because each definition is based upon certain key assumptions. We must therefore explore these assumptions.

The various perspectives on power, and the definitions derived from them, can be crudely divided into what might be called an *objective view* and a *subjective view*. Analysts adopting each of these views would probably agree that a power relation involves a conflict of interest between two or more parties. Furthermore, they would also probably agree that the resolution of this conflict is determined by the attributes that each party has at its disposal and the skill with which these attributes are deployed. Where an analyst taking an objective view of power parts company with one adopting a subjective view is on the approach that each takes to the concept of *interests*. This represents a crucial difference, because it directly delimits the range of circumstances in which power relationships are held to exist.

For writers adopting a subjective view, an actor's interests are held to be equivalent to expressed preferences or desires. Within this conception, a power relationship exists if actor A desires outcome x and actor B desires outcome y, and if A can achieve its preferred outcome against the explicit and direct opposition of B. The study of power within the subjective view thereafter entails an examination of those attributes that A or B might consciously deploy to secure their expressed preferences. Writers adopting an objective view claim, however, that this is not the only dimension to power, nor indeed the most important dimension. They contend that there are other aspects to power, that can only be highlighted once the definition of interests is expanded beyond the articulation of preferences. We share this latter view.

A critical element of the objective view is that interests are not always correctly perceived by those who attempt to articulate them. This is central to Lukes' work and that of his contemporary, Connolly. They have argued that interests may be distorted in a number of ways. Ignorance and the existence of social norms both alter preferences and obscure the recognition of needs. Beyond these structural distortions, interests are subject to conscious manipulation so that conflicts that might be expected to arise remain latent. The subjective approach is incapable of recognising this critical exercise of power.

Take for example a typical pay negotiation. If in such a negotiation you were unaware of the fact that all of your colleagues had been offered ten per cent and you thought that the average award was five per cent, this would affect your strategy. You might well respond positively to an offer of eight per cent, taking it as an indication of the value placed on your efforts. If somebody were to tell you how much others were receiving, however, then this would change everything.

Nonetheless, manipulation of interests through the careful management of information is a fact of everyday life. Indeed, such manipulation to gain a power advantage is particularly common in relations between buyers and suppliers. Economists did not, however, explicitly incorporate this factor into their thinking until the early 1960s. Since then economic models have recognised that if one of the participants in an exchange is unable to effectively monitor the position or actions of the other, the relatively informed party will probably take the opportunity to pursue their interests with guile. Central to this process of distortion are attempts to manipulate the expectations of the vulnerable party in ways that are least damaging to the manipulator.

The objective view generates certain methodological difficulties of its own, however. The analyst is presented with the problem of distinguishing an actor's real interest from one that is false, because the actor's expressed preferences cannot be taken at face value. It is easy for the researcher to spuriously ascribe particular interests to an actor, because he does not understand that actor's needs. Connolly asserted that one way out of this dilemma is to undertake a counterfactual conditional judgement about what an actor might *reasonably* be expected to want, were he or she aware of all of the alternatives and the costs and benefits that might be expected to flow from them. Under this conception, an option x can be held to be more in an actor's real interest than a second option y, if the actor, having experienced the results of both x and y, decides to choose option x.

Judgements about what an actor might reasonably be expected to want in the commercial context are of course complex. For the buyer, it is typical to talk in terms of value for money. This involves a series of complex trade-offs. The buyer has to make decisions about the appropriate mix of functionality and cost for the portfolio of goods and services that must be acquired. In theory, the rational buyer is concerned with obtaining the required level of functionality at the lowest possible cost, which means at cost. In this way, the supplier's gross profit margin is the key measure of the buyer's power. For the buyer, therefore, power is not about achieving the lowest *price*, but about its capacity to drive the supplier's returns on a transaction towards the long-run marginal cost of production.

For the supplier, on the other hand, power is used to push the level of return above long-run marginal cost, and, assuming there is repeat business, to hold it there. Given this definition of the buyer's objective interests, it is necessary for the buyer to know, with certainty, the supplier's costs of production. Conversely, if the supplier is to pursue its own objective interests, it is imperative that it conceals this same cost information. The extent to which there is an uneven distribution of cost information related to any given level of functionality between buyer and supplier is critical, therefore, to an understanding of both potential and actual power in exchange relationships. This uneven distribution is normally referred to as 'information asymmetry' in business-to-business relationships.

Another key feature of power is that it is *relative*. Power is not something like money that can be accumulated and stockpiled. In other words, no one firm has power in all contexts. Furthermore, a buyer-supplier exchange can never solely be about power, because there is always some measure of mutual interest between two contracting parties. The fact that firms are resource constrained means that they cannot do everything for themselves. They must, therefore, look to others to provide them with the goods and services that they are incapable of supplying for themselves. Thus, two contracting parties are dependent upon one another to the extent that each is able to offer the other something that it needs.

Recognising that a degree of mutual interest is a prerequisite of any buyer-supplier exchange is not the same, however, as saying that there is an equivalence of interest. Given that each firm is being offered something that it requires, and that each has to give up something in return, it is in their interests to ensure that the terms on which the exchange takes place offers them the maximum possible benefits. In order to achieve this, it is imperative that each firm is able to influence, or even control, the other's behaviour. Their capacity to do so will depend principally on the perceived ability of each contracting party to grant, hinder or deny the other's gratification relative to the other's perceived ability to do the same to them.

This was the core insight first arrived at by Richard Emerson in 1962. It was later applied to exchange networks by Emerson in conjunction with Cook, Gillmore and Yamagishi, and by Pfeffer and Salancik in the context of inter-organisational power relations. Both of these works demonstrate that this ability to grant, hinder or deny another's gratification is in turn reliant upon that party's dependency. It has been argued that such dependency is a function of two variables. These are the relative *utility* and the relative *scarcity* of the resources brought by each of the parties to an exchange relationship.

As Figure 1 shows, a buyer would have power over a supplier if two conditions held true. First, the buyer offers the supplier resources that are both relatively scarce and regarded by the supplier as having a relatively high utility. Secondly, the supplier's resources are relatively plentiful and are of relatively low utility for the buyer. Of course, if the exact opposite is true in terms of resource utility and scarcity, then logically the supplier must have power over the buyer.

Figure 1   *Potential Buyer and Supplier Business to Business Exchange Relationships*

		LOW	**HIGH**
Relative utility and scarcity of buyer's resources for supplier	**HIGH**	BUYER DOMINANCE	INTER-DEPENDENCE
	LOW	INDEPENDENCE	SUPPLIER DOMINANCE

Relative utility and scarcity of supplier's resources for buyer

The two remaining quadrants in Figure 1 represent those circumstances in which there is no power relation between the buyer and supplier. The buyer and supplier are said to be *interdependent* if the relative utility and scarcity of the resources held by each party are high. Finally, a situation of buyer-supplier *independence* is created where the relative utility and scarcity of the resources held by each party are low. The key question is how does one determine the relative magnitude of these variables in the context of a particular buyer-supplier relationship?

It is the answer to this question that forms the backbone of the next chapter. Specifically, we consider two issues. Firstly, we look at the contribution that scarcity, utility and information make to our understanding of power in business. Secondly, we begin to look at how an appreciation of these factors contributes in turn to a wider appreciation of supply chains and supply chain types.

CHAPTER **III**

MAPPING THE ATTRIBUTES OF POWER: THE DNA OF BUSINESS LIFE

We began this book by suggesting that there are parallels between biology and business. So, let us begin this chapter by reminding ourselves about them. And, what better place to start than with some of Hollywood's most famous people.

It's no accident that Cameron Diaz and Danny DeVito look as they do. An individual's physical appearance is determined by his, or her, genetic code. Cameron Diaz's code told her to grow tall and willowy, with beautiful eyes and a dazzling smile. Danny DeVito's code, on the other hand, dictated that he should be shorter, stouter and a little light in the hair department.

David Cronenberg, the American director, once mischievously observed that he would like to hold beauty contests based on people's physical interiors rather than their exteriors. Within such contests, the prizes would be awarded for one's spleen or liver rather than one's face or figure. So far, however, he has had no takers. This is perhaps not surprising, because our physical appearance plays a major part in shaping the value that others place on us. We might wish that this was not the case, but there is an abundance of evidence that tells us that it is.

Numerous psychological studies have shown that physical beauty is accompanied by a halo effect. That is, if we are perceived to excel physically, people also expect us to shine in other areas of our life. One such study of fifth grade pupils in Missouri classrooms found that teachers expected attractive people to be smarter, more outgoing and more popular with their peers than their less attractive counterparts. More disturbing still is that attractive students tend to do better in tests – unless, of course, their papers are marked blind.

Even more remarkable than the fact that beautiful people get a better deal out of life than less attractive people is the realisation that the basis for their advantage is so slim. Indeed, it rests on nothing more than a series of chemical interactions. Our DNA consists of two interlocking strands, which in turn is made up of a series of chemical compounds called nucleotides. These strands are arranged like a ladder that has been twisted to form the shape of a winding staircase often described as a double helix. Each nucleotide is made up of three units, a sugar, a phosphate and a base. There are four such bases – adenine (abbreviated to A), guanine (G), thymine (T), and cytosine (C) – and they act as the rungs of the ladder.

Each rung of the ladder consists of two bases, but their significance is not confined to the part that they play in joining the two strands together for it is these bases that literally tell the body how to build itself. This they do by providing the instructions for the production of proteins. A particular sequence of bases (the triplet GAC, for example) will direct the body to create one type of protein (in this instance, the amino acid leucine). A different sequence will lead to the production of a different type of protein (CAG is the code for valine). Shift the sequence of the bases around a little and an ugly duckling becomes a swan with all the aforementioned advantages.

Business is like biology in that some power structures benefit the firm more than others. It is obviously more beneficial for a firm to be dominant in relation to its customers and suppliers, than it is for it to be dependent. It is also normally more advantageous for the firm to be dominant rather than interdependent with its suppliers. This is because dominance offers the firm a flexibility in its dealings with customers and suppliers that interdependence does not. Thereafter, it is up to the firm how it uses this flexibility.

However, the similarity of business to biology does not end here. As with biology, the emergence of a particular power structure in business is not a random event. Rather, it is a direct function of the power base of the firm. Each side in a business related exchange relationship possesses certain resources that can augment or diminish the relative power of each player in the game. The balance of resources between the buyer and supplier in the exchange relationship, as we saw from the previous chapter, determines which of the four power categories will emerge to structure the process of exchange. These resources that shape which power category is likely to emerge fall into two main types (against the four of biology): *utility* and *scarcity*. Each of these bases (or attributes) of power is discussed below.

RESOURCE UTILITY

Resource utility is determined by two factors. The first factor is the *operational importance* of a particular resource in a business, while the second is the *commercial importance* of that resource to a firm's overall revenue generating activities. These factors must be addressed differently, however, depending on whether we are considering the buyer's or the supplier's perspective.

From a buyer's perspective, operational importance relates to the degree to which a particular resource (good or service) is indispensable to the provision of the firm's supply offering. This relates, in turn, to the number of *substitutes* that might readily replace the particular good or service. For example, access to a network infrastructure would constitute a resource of high operational importance for a provider of cable communication services. Without such a network the cable company cannot offer its services at all. However, many resources are of relatively low operational importance, because their absence or replacement would not prevent a firm from delivering its supply offering. For example, a firm may need competent managers, but it is not operationally essential for these managers to be provided with luxury company cars or ostentatious office surroundings.

From a supplier's perspective, however, the notion of operational importance is somewhat different, because the key (although not the only) resource in which a supplier is interested is a buyer's expenditure. Clearly, revenue cannot be assessed in terms of the degree to which it is indispensable to a finished good or service. Instead, we contend that the key determinant of the operational importance of a buyer's expenditure is the *regularity* and *predictability* of the buyer's expenditure.

It is axiomatic that business people, whether in their role as buyers or suppliers, have a preference for situations characterised by low degrees of uncertainty and complexity. Most people are, by their nature, risk averse. We can assume, therefore, that a supplier will have an operational preference for those buyers that can offer regular and predictable expenditure. A regular and predictable spend allows a supplier to make a credible commitment to future investment in R & D and capital equipment, as well as sustaining profitability. It is clear, however, that operational importance will be conditioned, not only by the predictability of demand, but also by the capacity of the supplier to generate 'acceptable returns' (profits) from any given level of regular and predictable demand.

This demonstrates the close relationship between operational and commercial importance. The capacity to generate 'acceptable returns' by the supplier is linked directly to the commercial importance of the buyer to the supplier's business. Here it is useful to adopt the line taken by Scott and Westbrook that the first determinant of commercial importance is the *ratio* between a buyer's expenditure with a particular supplier and that supplier's total sales revenue. Thus, if a buyer's expenditure is a relatively small proportion of the supplier's total sales revenue, then the buyer's expenditure will have a relatively low level of commercial importance for the supplier. If, however, the ratio of expenditure to total sales is higher, then the importance of the buyer's expenditure will increase commensurately.

The second determinant of commercial importance is not directly related to current revenue, but is associated with the future revenue generating opportunity presented to the supplier by having a relationship with a buyer. Suppliers know only too well that some relationships with particular buyers are 'highly attractive'. This is because the supplier can build future marketing strategy around its association with a highly prestigious buyer and anticipate a growth in the scale of its market share.

The fact that a resource, be it a good, a service or money, is of high commercial importance to a buyer or a supplier is not sufficient in itself, however, to give the resource a high utility for a particular firm. Firms are typically multi-business entities, active in a number of different markets, some of which are operationally and commercially more important than others. By this, we mean that some of the supply chains in which the firm is active contribute more than others to its revenues and profitability. Those areas that represent the bulk of the firm's revenue generating activities are described as *primary* activities, while the remainder are described as *support* activities. The relationship between the operational importance of a resource, its commercial importance, and the commensurate utility ascribed to that resource by the firm is illustrated in Figure 2.

Taking these factors into account it is possible to arrive at an understanding of the relative utility of any resource in buyer-supplier, business-to-business relationships. Figure 2 shows that for a resource to have a high utility for a particular buyer or supplier, in other words for it to be a *critical resource*, it must be both operationally and commercially important. Conversely, a *residual resource* is one that has a low utility for a particular buyer or supplier because it has a low operational importance and the transaction takes place in a support activity.

Figure 2 *The Relative Utility of Firm Resources*

	LOW Readily Substitutable	HIGH Non Substitutable
HIGH Primary activities	COMPLEMENTARY RESOURCE Low/ Medium Utility	CRITICAL RESOURCE High Utility
LOW Support activities	RESIDUAL RESOURCE Low Utility	KEY RESOURCE Medium/High Utility

Degree of Commercial Importance (vertical axis)

Degree of Operational Importance (horizontal axis)

Logically, there must, therefore, be two other types of resource utility. Those resources that have a low operational importance, but which occur in a primary area of activity, might be referred to as *complementary resources*. These resources will have low to medium utility for buyers and suppliers. Resources that have a high operational importance, but occur in support activity areas, might be referred to as *key resources*. These key resources will often have a high to medium utility because their high operational importance signifies that they are necessary and cannot easily be replaced by alternative resources.

RESOURCE SCARCITY

The second major attribute of buyer and supplier power is the relative scarcity of a resource. The scarcity of a resource is primarily determined by its *imitability* or its *substitutability*. In other words, if a resource is relatively easy and cheap to imitate or substitute, and it is in demand, then it is likely to be available from a large number of firms. Conversely, if a resource is difficult or expensive to imitate or substitute then the number of firms in possession of the resource is likely to be highly restricted. Such a resource would be imperfectly imitable or imperfectly substitutable and would, as a result, be relatively scarce.

A fundamental question to be asked about any buyer-supplier exchange is how many credible alternatives there are on either side of the association? A supplier needs to consider how likely it is to be able to replace a buyer's business with an exchange of equivalent utility, if it is not awarded the contract or if it loses the business. The answer to this question lies in a combination of the structure of the market into which the supplier is selling and its competitive position amongst potential suppliers. A buyer, on the other hand, needs to consider how many credible alternative suppliers there are for a particular good or service. Is the supply base highly restricted, or are there a large number of suitable suppliers?

If we are to develop a proper understanding of buyer and supplier power, however, we must go beyond these basic descriptive questions to seek explanations for the imperfect imitability or the imperfect substitutability of certain resources. There is an extensive literature in what is termed the 'resource-based' school of strategy that offers a range of explanations for these conditions. The degree to which a firm's competitive position is threatened by substitutes is, of course, a key part of Porter's well-known 'five forces' model. The vast majority of the work of the 'resource-based' school, however, has concerned the other issue - imperfect imitability.

One of the most important contributions to this debate was made by Rumelt. He developed the idea of 'isolating mechanisms' to refer to those factors that impede imitative competition and, thereby, create and maintain conditions of resource scarcity. These mechanisms are crucial for understanding why there may be only one, or a small number of buyers for particular goods or services. Equally, they help us to understand why particular goods or services can only be bought from one or a small number of suppliers.

Rumelt proposes two main types of isolating mechanisms: property rights to scarce resources and various quasi-property rights in the form of first-mover advantages. This second category includes information impactedness, buyer switching costs, reputation effects, buyer search costs, communication good effect, and economies of scale when specialised assets are required.

There is insufficient space in the context of this volume to discuss each of these mechanisms in detail. Instead, their key characteristics are shown in Table 1 and discussed at length in *Supply Chains, Markets and Power*. The key feature of these mechanisms is, however, that they create barriers to protect the unique market position of one, or a small number of firms. By doing this, they give buyers or suppliers dealing with the protected market few credible alternatives.

This lack of alternatives is a key power attribute for the firm or firms that are being protected.

Table 1 *Mechanisms that Impede Imitative Competition*

Mechanism	Characteristics
Property rights	The state or another legitimate authority (e.g. a firm) grants a licence or a patent to guarantee exclusive ownership or control of a relatively scarce resource for a specified period and under given conditions.
Economies of scale	If the minimum efficient scale of a business is comparable to the size of the market, and if the assets required are specialised to this use, a situation of natural monopoly occurs. Additional entrants would be unable to cover their fixed costs while pricing competitively.
Information impactedness	This means that the knowledge on which an innovation is based remains largely tacit and uncodified. It is difficult for potential competitors to obtain critical knowledge under these circumstances, unless a key employee decides to defect.
Causal ambiguity	This occurs if the basis of an innovation is particularly complex and 'path-dependent'. At the limit, even the innovating firm may be unable to trace the precise causality of its innovation. In these circumstances, imitation is impossible.
Reputation effect	Buyers cannot accurately evaluate many products and services until after they have been consumed. A supplier's reputation, therefore, plays a critical role in its ability to sell such 'experience' goods/services. First movers can obtain reputational advantages, because the strength of a supplier's reputation depends largely on the length of time that it has been providing satisfactory goods or services.
Buyer switching costs	If early buyers of a new product find it subsequently costly to switch to a competitor's offering then the first mover has an advantage. These costs are high when the buyer must make substantial dedicated investments in people or equipment in order to use the product.
Buyer search costs	These are high when the buyer is required to invest substantial amounts of time and money in understanding the complexities of different supply offerings. Firms seek to economise on these costs by free-riding on the presumed analyses of the well-informed and buying the market leader's product or service. This provides a first-mover advantage as long as followers' products are not significantly better.
Communication good effects	This effect arises when a product or service acts as a means of social co-ordination between different users (e.g. telephone networks, PC software). When a communication good is also an experience good, as in the case of software, then there is a need for standardisation and 'reputation bonding'. The first mover's product or service may thus become a *de facto* industry standard.
Collusive cartels	Under conditions of oligopoly firms often co-operate on sourcing, pricing and output decisions. Potential entrants are blocked by a co-ordinated response.

Adapted from Rumelt (1987)

However, resource scarcity can also be a function of an *information asymmetry* between firms involved in a vertical buyer-supplier relationship. Such asymmetries, as we noted earlier, are often a key part of power imbalances between buyers and suppliers. The notion of information asymmetry relates to the distinction that economists draw between public and private information. The former term refers to information that is either generally available or can be obtained by interested parties at relatively little cost. Private information, by contrast, represents hidden knowledge. In the context of a transaction, hidden knowledge is that which is known to just one of the contracting parties and which can only be obtained by the other through the expenditure of significant time and money, if at all.

Perhaps the best example of private information is a supplier's costs of production. When a transaction is undertaken under conditions of private information, the firm that owns or controls the information is able to use it as a source of scarcity. This scarcity results from the opportunistic exploitation of superior knowledge in one of two ways.

First, the privileged firm can use its superior knowledge to distort the other party's perception of the range of viable alternative firms with which it can undertake the transaction. For example, a firm buying highly complex IT services might not have the specialist knowledge needed to properly test the supply market. It might, therefore, award a contract simply on the basis of a supplier's reputation. This is often what buyers have to resort to in the case of 'credence goods', a term which refers to something that a buyer is incapable of evaluating even after it has been consumed. The buyer is therefore relying on the supplier to act honestly in providing value for money, which creates substantial room for opportunistic behaviour. When such opportunism occurs in the pre-contractual phase of a transaction it is referred to as *adverse selection*.

This kind of information asymmetry can also lead to the emergence of industry standard pricing. Under these circumstances, a buyer may believe that it is dealing with an open and competitive supply base. Nevertheless, suppliers are collectively able to price above the long-run average cost of production, because the buyer is ignorant of the true costs of the good or service that it is buying. This condition is particularly prevalent in the supply of consultancy and other professional services.

However, it is also possible for buyers to use privileged knowledge to gain an advantage in a similar manner. This is done by promising a supplier regular business in the future in order to get a better deal on a current contract. In this context, the information asymmetry relates to the buyer's superior knowledge of its projected spending. For such information-based leverage to be effective, however, a supplier must be convinced by the buyer's promises.

A privileged supplier can also use its superior knowledge to persuade the buyer to agree to contractual terms and conditions that constrain the range of options available to it in the future. It is not uncommon, for example, for a buyer to sign a five year framework agreement when a two year fixed term contract would have given it the necessary protection from opportunistic behaviour and the ability to re-contract should things go wrong. The supplier has used the relative uncertainty of the buyer to get guaranteed work for five years. More importantly, this is within a flexible framework agreement that allows the supplier to dictate the future requirements of its customer. Such post-contractual opportunism is known as *moral hazard*.

The potential leverage brought about by an information asymmetry between a buyer and a supplier is not, however, likely to be as effective, or as durable, as that derived from property rights to relatively scarce resources or quasi-property rights in the form of first-mover advantages. As Oliver Williamson, possibly the most eminent academic writer in this area today, argues, a buyer or a supplier should be able to avoid long-term dependency on an opportunistic supplier, or customer, through a combination of experiential learning and the adoption of a governance structure with appropriate safeguards.

Nevertheless, for those buyers or suppliers without the chance to acquire relatively scarce resources based on property rights or first mover advantages, the effective exploitation of information asymmetries can often prove to be a fruitful secondary strategy. Indeed, a recent study of outsourcing by Lonsdale and Cox found ample evidence of suppliers using the relative ignorance of buyers to create situations of lock-in, particularly when the buyer is required to make substantial dedicated investments to support the transaction. The study found that this type of dependency is particularly prevalent in the outsourcing of bespoke and specialist services such as IT.

Whether or not a buyer or seller possess particular resources that have scarcity or utility value for the other party to the exchange will over-determine the power in the relationship between the two parties. This process is analogous to the way in which biological bases come together to create the genetic code that determines specific characteristics in an organism. Instead of creating webbed-feet, a trunk or an exoskeleton, however, the relative utility and scarcity value of particular resources in an exchange relationship will create either a situation of *buyer dominance, interdependence, independence* or *supplier dominance* in a particular part of a supply chain. And, just as certain biological characteristics shape the effectiveness with which specific life forms interact with their environment, these power structures impact on the commercial success of the firms directly involved in the exchange relationship.

It must be recognised, however, that a firm will not have just one category of relationship with its dyadic customers and suppliers. All firms develop a wide range of dyadic power relationships with a multitude of different customers and suppliers – each of whom have their own unique power resources.

To focus only on dyadic relationships is however myopic. What lean thinking tells us, if nothing else, is that a commercial focus needs to be much wider than this. Many seemingly intractable problems with suppliers originate not from the immediate supplier, but rather from the supplier's suppliers upstream. Similarly, changes in the commercial climate downstream are nearly always fed back along the supply chain, and sometimes with catastrophic effect. A firm that does not have an eye on what is happening with its upstream and downstream relationships is likely, therefore, to be overtaken by events. If practitioners are to master the world of upstream and downstream relationship management it is our view they need to understand its geography better – certainly better than many currently do.

Our next chapter turns to look at this world in more detail and it does so by extending the perspective that we have tried to develop in the previous two. If one buyer-supplier relationship represents one element in a supply chain, what happens when you start to combine these elements? In biology if you combine them you create a unique organism with unique capabilities. But what does uniqueness mean in supply chain terms?

36

CHAPTER IV

BLUE EYES AND BROWN HAIR: MAKING SENSE OF SUPPLY CHAIN INDIVIDUALITY

What makes an individual unique is the combination of his or her constituent parts, none of which are necessarily unusual in themselves but which, when taken together, provide a human being's individuality. There are many people born with blond hair (not to mention those who acquire their blond hair out of a bottle), but there are somewhat fewer numbers of people with blond hair and blue eyes. There are fewer still with blond hair, blue eyes, a small nose and perfectly formed teeth. Of those with these characteristics, however, none are exactly the same.

Supply chains are the same in that no two are identical. Even firms offering very similar products or services to very similar markets will not necessarily share all the same customers and all the same suppliers. And, even if they did, their respective power positions would still, in all probability, be different.

It follows, therefore, that attempting to characterise types of supply chains is rather like trying to characterise types of human beings – it cannot be done simply or descriptively if one still hopes to do justice to the subject. Just as it is possible to talk descriptively about human beings in terms of whether they are men or women, tall or short, thin or fat, it is also possible to talk descriptively about supply chains. Supply chains can produce goods or services; they can be innovative or static and they can be project based or process orientated.

The problem is, whether we are talking about human beings or supply chains, none of the characteristics described above tell us very much about the motives, aspirations or capabilities of the human beings or supply chains that we are describing. What we really need is ways of thinking analytically and predictively about what human beings, or supply chains, are capable of doing or becoming. When we talk about human beings this would equate to us being able to make predictions about the type of person an individual is, and how they are likely to behave under particular circumstances. This is akin to saying that a person is hard working or lazy, kind or cruel, morose or happy, altruistic or selfish.

When we apply this way of thinking to supply chains it means that we are searching for a way of thinking that allows us to make analytic and predictive statements about how a supply chain can be managed, and how relationships should be organised to achieve particular valued outcomes. This would be equivalent to being able to say that one supply chain is, or is not, conducive to an integrated supply chain management approach. Or that a particular supply chain has a power structure that lends itself to short-term and agile adversarial opportunism rather than long-term non-adversarial, collaborative relationship building. But how is one to arrive at this predictive and analytic approach to supply chain analysis?

Our view is that the answer to this question is simple enough if one starts from first principles in building an analytical picture of any supply chain. Rather than trying to look at the big picture all at once and then encapsulate all of the diversity of a supply chain in just a few words, a better approach is to look at the constituent elements of the chain individually and then piece them together like a jigsaw. Then, the question becomes, not what type of supply chain is this descriptively, but what, analytically, is the *power regime* that has to be managed in the extended network of dyadic buyer and supplier exchange relationships in the chain?

This chapter attempts to explain how to begin this way of thinking by first looking at a simple supply chain and its *power regime*. Having explained how a simple supply chain *power regime* is analysed we move on to explain how the *power regimes* that exist in more complicated supply chain networks can be analysed.

POWER IN SIMPLE REGIMES

Figure 3 is made up of 16 highly stylised buyer-supplier exchanges. They each represent a *power regime*. Each regime is comprised of two interlocking buyer-supplier relationships, which we call A–B and B–C. Here the reader should not be intimidated by the rather technical-looking use of symbols. It might look like maths, but it is not. It is just a short hand to accompany the description – so the reader can see more clearly, which regime we are talking about.

Each of the buyer-supplier relationships, which we will call dyads from now on, is categorised according to the power relation that exists within it. That is, according to whether the exchange is characterised by *buyer dominance (or power), supplier dominance (or power), buyer-supplier interdependence* or *buyer-supplier independence*. In the figure, the existence of *buyer power* is indicated by the symbol (A > B or B > C); *supplier power* by (A < B or B < C); *buyer-supplier interdependence* by (A = B or B = C); and *buyer-supplier independence* by (A 0 B or B 0 C).

These 16 regimes are divided into four groups on the basis of the power relation that exists between A and B. This is described in the text as the downstream relationship. It is called this because physically, goods and services are being passed from the firm (B), down the chain to its customer (A). It is rather like a river flowing, down into the sea.

Group 1 contains those regimes where A has power over B (A > B). Group 2 contains those regimes where A and B are interdependent (A = B). Group 3 contains those regimes where A and B are independent of one another (A 0 B). Finally, Group 4 contains those regimes where B has power over A (A < B). We have then placed four regimes within each of these four groups, on the basis of the power relation that exists between B and C. Each one of the four possible power relations between B and C is represented in each group. We refer to this as the upstream relationship, because the firm (B) stands between the source (C) and its final destination (A). This leads to the generation of 16 exchange regimes in total.

BLUE EYES AND BROWN HAIR   41

Figure 3 *Value Appropriation in Double-Dyad Exchange Regimes*

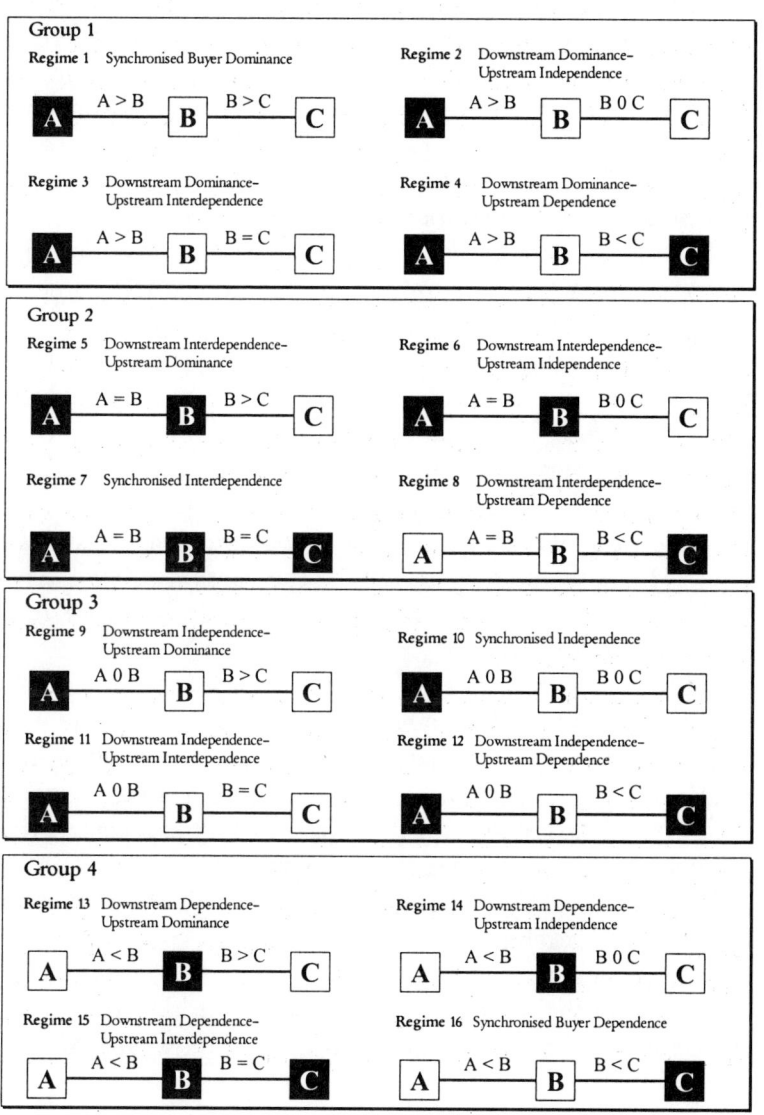

The flow of value between exchange partners is held to operate according to the following set of rules. Where a situation of *buyer power* or of *buyer–supplier independence* exists, we contend that value flows from the supplier to the buyer (B to A, or C to B). In the context of *independence*, this occurs because competition in either B's or C's marketplace is forcing them to offer their respective customers a good deal. If they don't, their customers will go elsewhere.

In the context of *buyer dominance*, value flows to the customer because the supplier has few alternatives for its products. Where a situation of *supplier power* exists, we contend that value flows from the buyer to the supplier (A to B, or B to C). Again, the reason for this should be obvious. If there is no real choice in the supply market, or if firms in the supply market are co-operating to fix prices, then its/their customers would not expect to get the best possible deal. Where a situation of *interdependence* exists, we contend that the pains and gains of the relationship will tend to be shared. In effect, this type of power structure best supports the lean ideal.

Those actors within each regime that are in a position to appropriate and accumulate the available value are represented by a black square, while those from which the value is being appropriated are shown as a white square. This is to make it easier for the reader to spot at a glance, the winners and losers from each *power regime*.

It is unnecessary to describe the exchange characteristics of all of the different power regimes shown in Figure 3. By just describing a few examples the reader should be able to work out on their own what is happening in the remainder. A more detailed exposition is provided, however, in the longer companion volume to this book, *Supply Chains, Markets and Power*.

Listed in the order that they appear, the regimes that will be discussed are Regime 10 (*Synchronised Independence*), Regime 7 (*Synchronised Interdependence*), Regime 13 (*Downstream Dependence-Upstream Dominance*), and Regime 4 (*Downstream Dominance-Upstream Dependence*). As we shall see, the selection of these four types is not undertaken randomly, but rather is a reflection of the particular and important type of business context that each highlights.

If one were to turn to an economics textbook to find out what the *power regime* in a supply chain ought to look like, it would soon be obvious that this issue is not addressed. However, if one were to extrapolate from what the textbook says about dyadic relationships, the reader would soon find that the *power regime* would approximate to Regime 10, *Synchronised Independence*. Economists like to conceive of economic relationships taking place in an ideal world, comprised of many interlocking markets, which in turn are inhabited by a myriad of buyers and sellers. Furthermore, in this ideal world information would be relatively costless and easy to obtain. Under such circumstances firms would be forced to compete constantly just to survive.

This is because in such a market, with information so easy to obtain, any supply innovation would be easily copied and the value to the firm that created it would be quickly dissipated. Furthermore, in a world of free information, opportunism would be impossible. The opportunistic behaviour of the would-be cheat would easily be spotted and any such firms would quickly lose their business with any of the customers or suppliers of which they tried to take advantage. They would also probably lose their reputation into the bargain, as word got around.

In such a world, value always passes to the end-customer. If C is not prepared to delight B or if B is not prepared to delight A, then the buyer in each case, will find a firm that will. Therefore, C passes value to B and B then passes it onto A.

Fortunately for the firm, however, the economist's model is something of a rarity. What entrepreneur would want to speculate in an environment where it was guaranteed that their profits would quickly fall towards zero. There are some observers who would actually go so far as to say that it describes an environment that has never, will never and could never exist.

More common is the circumstance in which, despite the existence of many buyers and many sellers, one side still has certain informational advantages over the other party. In a world where there is no customer loyalty (because there is such a wide choice of suppliers), but in which information is not freely available, people will learn to cheat. Indeed, in such an environment, opportunism becomes a commercial necessity. Suppliers are forced to inflate prices as a hedge, so that they can bring them down again if it looks like they will lose a contract and they need to win back the business. Without such a hedge, the firm has no fallback position.

Similarly, the supplier may not make available all of the innovation that they might. Once again, the hope would be to offer it when it was most needed. Certainly, without the guarantee of repeat business, many firms will be reluctant to invest in their customers.

This is what lean thinkers say has happened in many Western markets. The difficulty with such an approach, they claim, is that when firms are finally exposed to competition from markets where opportunism and hedging has not been the norm, they find themselves considerably behind the productivity frontier. In the place of opportunism lean supply offers co-operation. Where interdependency exists, where continuity of relationship is guaranteed, the requirement to hedge is eradicated.

Furthermore, the ability to do so is also removed. In an interdependency information is exchanged and when this happens it is difficult to cheat without getting caught. Instead of confronting each other, the participants in a lean enterprise work together to improve the position of everyone associated with the network. 'All for one and one for all' might well be the motto. The regime that probably most closely describes this circumstance is Regime 7, *Synchronised Interdependence*.

In Regime 7 (A = B = C), the value is shared equally, because each of the parties is dependent upon the other. A is dependent upon B, which is in turn dependent upon A. In the same way, B is dependent upon C, which is in turn dependent upon B. Consequently, A and C are also interdependent, because if either party fails, B would suffer equally.

One problem with this regime type is that it may not be the most profitable position for the firm to be in. It is almost certain that it will not be the most flexible. *Interdependence* requires the firm to share and consult. If £100 is saved through co-operation, a fair allocation would be one third to each of the participants. This would be one third that might not otherwise have been available in an arms-length adversarial existence, but it is two-thirds less that the firm would have got if it had configured the supply chain so that it could engineer the savings and keep all of them for itself.

Similarly, *interdependence* is a discipline. Parties cannot just do what they want, but must proceed through mutual consent. Compromise is not a dirty word, but it is definitely a difficult one and sometimes a dangerous one. Sometimes the firm needs to follow its own path, whatever the consequences for others. *Interdependence* places restriction on the pursuit of self-interest.

This is why most business strategy writing tends to see the world in a rather different way. Regime 13, *Downstream Dependence-Upstream Dominance* (A < B > C), in which a firm B, is able to leverage both its supplier and customer relationships to appropriate the bulk of the value, probably comes closest to the model developed by Michael Porter in his 1980 book, *Competitive Strategy*. Conversely, the *Downstream Dominance-Upstream Dependence* illustrated in Regime 4 (A > B < C) probably comes closest to Porter's model of business failure. Certainly, in such a regime, firm B would be the net loser.

POWER IN COMPLEX REGIMES

The double-dyad exchange regimes discussed above provide a rather stylised version of how supply chain power relationships actually operate. It is possible, however, to apply the same rules to a more sophisticated representation of a supply chain. In Figure 4, we have constructed two hypothetical supply chain power regimes. These are based on the linkage of dyadic exchange relationships consisting of eight agents (A, B, C, D, E, F, G and H).

We have joined these agents together by means of seven exchange dyads (A–B, B–C, C–F, B–D, D–G, B–E and E–H) to create a complex network of relationships linked together to create goods and/or services for end customers. In effect, these could be seen as supply chains consisting of an end customer (A), an assembler (B), three components suppliers (C, D and E) and three suppliers of raw materials (F, G and H).

In both of these hypothetical supply chain power regimes the B–C relation (B > C), the C–F relation (C > F), the B–D relation (B < D), the D–G relation (D = G), the B–E relation (B = E) and the E–H relation (E 0 H) remain fixed. The only difference between the two networks is the A–B relation. Two of the four possible dyadic exchange circumstances are mapped on to this relationship in each power regime. *Buyer dominance* and *buyer–supplier independence* are grouped together in Supply Chain Power Regime 1, while *supplier dominance and buyer–supplier interdependence* are grouped together in Supply Chain Power Regime 2. As we will explain later, the dyadic exchange circumstances have been grouped together in this particular way, because, in the context of each of these *power regimes* as a whole, they lead to the same value appropriation outcomes.

In both of the *power regimes* shown, the value flows from F to C to B as a result of the series of cascading power relationships that operate to B's advantage. Like a series of Russian dolls, C appropriates value from F, only to see this value in turn appropriated by B. Similarly, in the double-dyad exchange regime containing B, E and H, E is able to appropriate value from H by virtue of the *independent* relationship between them. E must then share at least some of this value with B, because these two actors do business on the basis of an *interdependent* exchange relationship.

Figure 4   *Value Appropriation in Complex Power Regimes*

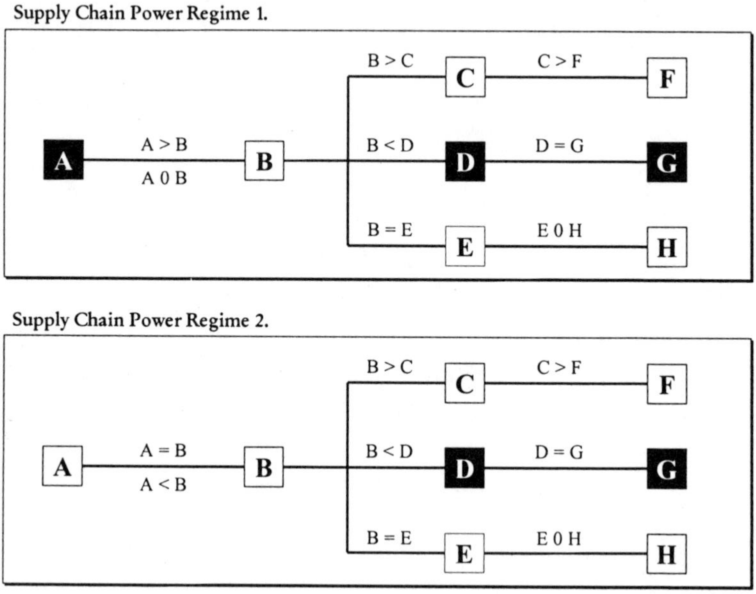

Supply Chain Power Regime 1.

```
                        B > C              C > F
                    ┌────── C ────────────── F
          A > B     │  B < D              D = G
    A ──────────  B ┼────── D ────────────── G
          A 0 B     │  B = E              E 0 H
                    └────── E ────────────── H
```

Supply Chain Power Regime 2.

```
                        B > C              C > F
                    ┌────── C ────────────── F
          A = B     │  B < D              D = G
    A ──────────  B ┼────── D ────────────── G
          A < B     │  B = E              E 0 H
                    └────── E ────────────── H
```

In both networks, however, B's grip on the value that it appropriates from each of these double-dyad exchange regimes is at best only tenuous. This is because, in the remaining double-dyad exchange regime (containing B, D and G), B is *dependent* on D and is, therefore, likely to be leveraged by D. At the same time, D's *interdependence* with G means that the benefits that D derives from its association with B are likely to be shared with G.

As we can see, therefore, the value appropriation outcomes on the supply (upstream) side of the assembler (B) are the same in both of our hypothetical exchange networks. The principal difference between the networks relates to the exchange circumstances that exist between B and its end customer (A). In Supply Chain Power Regime 1, B is assumed either to be *dependent* upon A (A > B) or to have an *independent* relationship with A (A 0 B). In both of these exchange circumstances, B is forced to pass value to A by pricing its product at or near the cost of production.

Consequently, in Supply Chain Power Regime 1, B is being leveraged both by its customer and by one of its major component suppliers (D). Any value that B is able to appropriate in its relationships with C and E is therefore immediately passed on to A (in the form of low prices) and D (in the form of inflated bought–in costs). The profit margin being earned by B in these circumstances is likely to be extremely low.

The value appropriation outcome from the A–B relation in Supply Chain Power Regime 2 is radically different. In this case, B is assumed either to be *interdependent* with its customer or to have power over A. As the diagram shows, however, the value appropriation outcome under both of these exchange circumstances is a function of B's dependence on D. Thus, where A and B are *interdependent* with one another, A is forced to share in the exploitation being visited on B by D. All of the value created by the association between A and B is appropriated by D, which then shares this value with G.

Conversely, where A is dependent upon B, B is able to appropriate value from A by charging a price that is significantly above its cost of production. Nevertheless, B cannot retain this value in the form of higher margins, because it must pay the inflated prices being charged by D. As before, D shares the value that it appropriates from B with G.

It seems clear, therefore, that this approach to analysing the dyadic relationships that operate between buyers and suppliers in the complex networks of exchange adds an additional level of understanding to many of the current descriptive approaches towards supply chain categorisation. It should also suggest that there is a significant potential for power imbalances in buyer-supplier relationships to undermine the search by practitioners for integrated supply chain management solutions.

The reasons for this are self-evident. If operational efficiency is to be achieved in a supply chain, then the flow of inputs from raw materials to the assembled good or service needs to be effectively co-ordinated. All too often, however, the requisite level of co-ordination cannot be achieved, because supply chains are characterised by *power regimes* that are hostile to an uninterrupted flow of value from the end customer to raw material providers. It is for partly this reason – the self-regarding efforts of some supply chain actors to appropriate value – that so many attempts at integrated supply chain management have failed, and will continue to do so. And, it is to this issue of appropriate business management in supply chain relationships that we now turn.

CHAPTER V

LOVE AND MARRIAGE IN SUPPLY CHAINS

Roses are red
Violets are blue
It's because of our respective Deoxyribonucleic acids
That I am proposing to you

There are many different types of relationship. Professionally, people have many contacts and acquaintances. These are people that you might see from time to time. Some of these people you get on with, while others you do not. There may be others to whom you will be quite indifferent. How you choose to conduct these relationships is another matter. We all know people who are quite curt with those that they do not know well. Other people that we meet are unfailingly polite to us and to others. Some relationships are closer in that they reflect a more frequent interaction. Again, however, some people conduct these types of relationships in different ways. They may be cordial (and even loving) or they may be distant and hostile. Many long-term relationships are abusive.

The issue of the regularity with which we meet particular people and how we conduct ourselves when we do is an interesting one. From a very early age we learn that certain types of behaviour are inappropriate under certain circumstances. We might be cordial with somebody who we had never met before and were never likely to meet again, but we would not pretend that they were our best friend with whom we would share our deepest intimacies. On the other hand, few of us would choose to verbally abuse close colleagues, particularly if they are senior to us. It just is not good politics.

This last point is particularly pertinent because it suggests that beyond the question of whether or not we like someone, instrumental considerations also play a part in determining how we conduct ourselves. This instrumentalism permeates even some of our closest ties. We have already suggested that there are advantages to being beautiful (and it must be admitted, disadvantages too). Being beautiful is to increase one's value in another's eyes.

But why should this be the case? The answer is likely to have something to do with our genetic programming. Our genetic code is telling us to find the best available genetic stock with which to reproduce, because it is the output of this stock that stands the best chance of survival in a hostile world. Our brains might not be making this mental calculation. When we look at someone, we just see an attractive face. However, we find that face attractive for a reason and that reason is the 'healthy' associations that we make with it.

However, while we may all find the same sorts of people attractive – psychological testing has shown that whatever people might say, the notion that beauty is in the eye of the beholder has only limited credibility – our chances of getting what we want might be quite limited. Beautiful people have more options and face greater levels of temptation than plain people do. That is why when people marry they tend to end up with someone who possesses similar levels of attractiveness to their own. Trying to forge a life-partnership involving two people with really quite marked differences in physical attractiveness will always prove problematic unless the deficient party can compensate their mate in other areas. Money, a sense of humour or a good heart are often cited as such balancing mechanisms.

Of course, similarities in physical attractiveness may not guarantee a stable outcome in relationships, but they probably contribute to the chances of it. And, because it is our genetic code that shapes our bodies, it is two people's respective DNA that plays a major role in their love lives.

Business partnerships tend to flourish for the same sorts of reason. There is a lot of talk in the business management literature about partnerships (what one might describe as a commercial marriage). While it is true that all commercial relationships have to be worked at, it also helps if the two organisations start with similar levels of resource endowment (or power-DNA). Moreover, it is imperative that each party possesses a high motivational investment in the other's fortunes. Specifically, for the partnership to work, *interdependence* is required. The two parties must be in love. An *independent* or footloose attitude just will not cut it.

Firms should also be aware that just as in social relations, where individuals come together in a wide range of contexts, and can behave towards each other in a variety of different ways, the same is true for business. Furthermore, while there may a wide range of different ways in which firms can conduct themselves in business, particular types of commercial behaviour will only work well under particular circumstances. The language of collaboration, trust and partnership are fine in principle, but they need the right structures of power to support them. We dedicate this chapter, therefore, to saying a few words about what types of buyer-supplier relationship are available to us, and when it is right to use them.

The practitioner has two choices to make about how any relationship should be managed. The first choice concerns the way in which the relationship will be managed. Will it be managed closely and collaboratively, with a high degree of trust and mutual sharing of information? Or will it be managed at arm's-length, with few opportunities for close information exchange? This we might call *the way of working* that will be used within the relationship.

The second factor relates to the choice over how the spoils from the creation of the relationship will be shared. As we have seen, business-to-business relationships are normally formed in order to create value and to generate profits for each of the parties to an exchange. It does not follow, however, that just because a relationship is created, that the share of value to the parties in the exchange will always be equal, although it may be.

Rather it is better to accept that the share of value appropriated by either of the parties to any exchange may vary from 0% to 100%. This continuum can, for ease of presentation, be simplified into two basic choices. In the first, the share of value may be split on the basis of equality (50/50). On the other hand, the value appropriated may be allocated on the basis of inequality between the two parties to the exchange. The most adversarial form of allocation between a buyer and a supplier is normally referred to as a zero-sum conflict, in which one party receives 100% of what is created and the other receives 0%.

LOVE AND MARRIAGE   55

These variables when brought together create four basic relationship management choices, which are outlined in the diagram below (Figure 5). Recognition of the basic choices is an important insight. This is because, as will be shown later, it allows us to understand why so much of the recent writing and practice around the concept of close collaborative 'partnerships' is misguided.

As the diagram demonstrates, there are a number of relationship management choices available to the practitioner, whether the party involved is a buyer or a supplier. In the top left quadrant (*an adversarial arm's-length relationship*), the buyer or supplier is interested only in forming a relationship that will allow them to keep the other party in the exchange at arm's-length. In this relationship there will be limited sharing of information or resources and an intention of allowing the other party only a very low share of the value created from the exchange.

In the bottom left quadrant (*a non-adversarial arm's-length relationship*) the buyer or supplier is less concerned about appropriating all of the value for themselves, and may be prepared to forego the maximisation of profitability in exchange for other benefits. There is still, however, no real desire for the way of working to remain anything other than arm's-length, with a limited sharing of sensitive information and resources.

In the top right hand quadrant (*an adversarial collaborative relationship*), the buyer or supplier is interested in working closely with the other party to the exchange, and is keen to share sensitive and confidential information and resources. Despite this, the buyer or supplier is not intending to have to countenance an equal sharing of the value created, but is rather seeking to appropriate the maximum share of the value for themselves.

In the final quadrant (*a non-adversarial collaborative relationship*), the buyer or supplier is interested in a close collaborative relationship, with a sharing of sensitive and confidential information and resources. The buyer or supplier also recognises the need to share the value created on the basis of relative equality. This type of relationship is what is often referred to as a 'partnership'.

Figure 5   *Relationship Portfolio Analysis*

	Arm's-Length	Collaborative
Inequality	ADVERSARIAL ARM'S-LENGTH RELATIONSHIP	ADVERSARIAL COLLABORATIVE RELATIONSHIP
Equality	NON-ADVERSARIAL ARM'S-LENGTH RELATIONSHIP	NON-ADVERSARIAL COLLABORATIVE RELATIONSHIP

Relative Share of Value Appropriation (vertical axis)

Way of Working (horizontal axis)

(Source: Robertson Cox Ltd, 1998 All Rights Reserved)

Given this segmentation of relationship management choices, it becomes transparent that the development of appropriate relationship management strategies by buyers and suppliers must be based on three factors. The first factor is *the power situation* within which each party finds itself, based on the relative utility and scarcity of the resources involved in the exchange. The second factor is a sophisticated awareness *of the range of relationship management strategies* that are available for appropriating value and for working with others.

The third, and perhaps the most important factor, however, is *judgement.* Judgement refers to the buyer's/supplier's ability to choose the appropriate type of relationship management strategy so as to maximise the appropriation of value under the particular circumstances of power and opportunity that exist at any given moment of time.

The problem, of course, is that buyers and suppliers do not always possess all of the information they need to be able to properly understand the power and opportunity circumstances in which they are operating. As a result, they often make certain decisions about which relationship management strategies to adopt that they would not have done if they had known more. Conversely, many practitioners and their advisers do not understand the full range of relationship management choices that are available.

As a result, it is not uncommon for people to benchmark the actions of others, and to copy the successful practices they see, even though the power and opportunity circumstances facing them are not the same. Or they come to believe that one particular approach is being used, even though the case they are analysing is in fact an example of a completely different relationship management approach. They then adopt a strategy based on a fundamental misunderstanding of the actual relationship approach being adopted by the exemplar companies that they are analysing.

It is our view that much of the analysis undertaken by the lean school of thinking is based on this latter analytic weakness and that, as a result, many of the recent attempts by Western companies to replicate Japanese supply chain and relationship management practices suffer from these problems. The current penchant for encouraging 'partnership' or integrated supply chain management strategies as the key to business success demonstrates a clear lack of awareness of the circumstances of power and opportunity that exist in many of the supply chains being analysed. Relatedly, there is also evidence that commentators and practitioners are recommending the adoption of an inappropriate relationship management strategy, namely non-adversarial collaboration.

Space precludes a fulsome discussion of the issues raised here, but suffice it to say that the key problem in the effective operationalisation of supply chain (buyer and supplier) management appears to reside in a simplistic attachment to two views. The first view is that all supply chain relationships are alike, which they are not. The second is that one approach to relationship management, non-adversarial collaboration, is the appropriate way to manage most, if not all, supply chain relationships in all circumstances.

The real problem appears to be that Western observers of business practice in the automotive sector have recognised that buyers in Japan have historically adopted a more collaborative approach to suppliers than the traditional arm's-length approach used in the West. Unfortunately this correct description of Japanese practice has not been matched by a sufficiently sophisticated analysis of the relationship management style being adopted in Japan. Western commentators do not appear to have understood that there is a significant difference between *adversarial-collaborative* and *non-adversarial collaborative* business to business relationships.

Leading writers in this area appear to have mistakenly associated collaborative working practices with relative equality in value appropriation, without recognising that the Japanese model has always been based on *adversarial collaborative* relationships associated with *buyer dominance*. Unfortunately, it would now appear that these same writers, having made this initial analytical error, have now compounded their mistake. In most of their recent work they have argued that the key to strategic and operational success for all companies in all types of supply chains is the adoption of *non-adversarial collaborative* relationships between buyers and suppliers.

Given this, it is hardly surprising that most of the evidence being recorded by practitioners and academics about the benefits of these types of 'partnership' relationship, reveals that many of the much-vaunted benefits are illusory. This is particularly true of those benefits associated with the sharing of innovation over the long-term.

Furthermore, there is a growing body of evidence in the outsourcing literature that suggests that, in some circumstances, the practice of developing close collaborative long-term supply relationships can actually be highly damaging to the effective control of quality and cost. Studies by Lonsdale and Cox, and Lacity and Willcocks, both show this. This conclusion is unsurprising to us, because it is clear that what is being recommended to practitioners, whether they be buyers or suppliers, is often based on a lack of understanding of appropriateness in the choice of relationship management approaches in particular circumstances of power and opportunity.

There is insufficient space here to explain fully the way in which a rigorous methodology might be developed to assist practitioners with the specification of appropriate relationship management choices. In the space that remains, however, the first steps that must be taken by practitioners can be outlined.

The first requirement is for practitioners to recognise that they must understand as objectively as possible the circumstances of power and opportunity that exist. To achieve this, practitioners must understand the appropriate questions that they need to ask of the circumstances in which they find themselves. They must also understand the potential opportunities that might arise in the future, in terms of the costs and benefits for themselves and for those with whom they establish exchange relationships.

Obviously, the questions that must be asked are complex, vary with specific exchange relationships, and cannot be fully outlined here. Despite this, it is clear that the first step in developing appropriateness in judgement is always to develop an understanding of the relative utility and scarcity of resources in the exchange between a buyer and a supplier. If this is achieved, then it will be possible to arrive at an understanding of the current, and future, power and opportunity positions that face both parties to an exchange relationship.

The second requirement is to link these power circumstances with the relationship management choices shown earlier in Figure 5.

Figure 6 *Power and Relationship Management Matrix*

Buyer Dominance (BDOM)	BDOM-1	BDOM-2	BDOM-3	BDOM-4
Interdependence (INT)	INT-1	INT-2	INT-3	INT-4
Independence (IND)	IND-1	IND-2	IND-3	IND-4
Supplier Dominance (SDOM)	SDOM-1	SDOM-2	SDOM-3	SDOM-4
	Type 1 Adversarial Arms-Length	Type 2 Non-Adversarial Arms-Length	Type 3 Adversarial Collaborative	Type 4 Non-Adversarial Collaborative

(Source: Robertson Cox Ltd, 1999 All Rights Reserved)

As Figure 6 demonstrates, the problem for the buyer or supplier in any exchange relationship is that there is no simple connection between the type of power and opportunity circumstance in which they find themselves, and the most appropriate type of relationship through which to manage this circumstance. This is because buyers and suppliers can choose any one of the four approaches to relationship management in any of the four power and opportunity circumstances outlined.

Whichever relationship management choice a practitioner makes in any power and opportunity circumstance, they will discover that the selection made has a range of outcomes, some beneficial and some not so beneficial. The test of competence for practitioners, and for those who seek to advise them, is not simply to be able to recognise that there are four power and opportunity circumstances in which they might find themselves.

The real test of competence is an ability to be able to answer a key question. This is, which of the four possible buyer-supplier relationship scenarios is most appropriate under particular power and opportunity circumstances? This implies the ability to specify clearly what costs and benefits might arise for a buyer or a supplier when they choose to operate in any one of the four relationship management scenarios that are available.

Only when the practitioner has understood the true costs and benefits of operating in any one of these four scenarios, is it possible for him to make a judgement about appropriateness. Appropriateness refers to the ability of a practitioner to understand and to monitor the effectiveness with which any particular relationship management approach delivers a desired outcome, in relation to value appropriation within a particular configuration of power and opportunity. Such a view implies that competence requires an iterative approach to power and relationship management, because circumstances are contingent and continually change in power and opportunity terms.

As circumstances change, the relationship management choice that a buyer or a supplier makes will also have to change according to the perceived costs and benefits that are delivered due to the adoption of any particular approach.

What is meant by this can be illustrated by reference to the case studies that follow. They show how buyers and suppliers might utilise the four possible relationship management approaches that we have identified, to their advantage or to their disadvantage.

CHAPTER **VI**

MAKING CHOICES AND LEARNING TO LIVE WITH THEM

In life, we all have to make choices. Some of them will be major and some of them will be minor. That is, some of them will be life altering, while others will not seem to change the general direction of our lives at all. Buying a new house is obviously a big deal. It seems an even bigger deal if we do not choose wisely and buy a lemon. There is a Tom Hanks film in which a young couple buy their dream home only to find it falling down around their ears. A great deal of humour is to be had out of their disintegrating house and the relationship that follows it. For anybody who has ever been placed in this position, of course, the humour concerned is gallows humour. In contrast to buying a dream house, choosing whether to have one lump of sugar in one's tea or two lumps, hardly seems to matter.

That said, 'seems' is an important caveat. Many of the most significant events in our lives will have started out small. How many people first met their future partner at a bar. How often in such cases was it just luck that both parties opted to go to that bar on that particular night.

Whether or not we understand the significance of our actions at the time, we have to learn to live with them. In this penultimate chapter, we look at four examples of the choices that particular firms made at particular points in their existence. Each case shows the alternative paths that individual firms opted to take under different circumstances. Each case also reveals some of the consequences of these choices.

All of the examples that are covered represent choices that turned out to be significant – whether or not the parties understood this at the time. The first case illustrates this point well in that it represents perhaps one of the greatest mistakes in recent business history. And the size of that mistake can be measured in terms of the turnover of the company that it helped to create. That company was Microsoft and the company that miscalculated was IBM.

CASE A: THE QUICK-FIX SUPPLY CASE

This is the case of a historically dominant buyer attempting to manage a supply relationship on the basis of an *adversarial arms-length* relationship, when in fact it should have used an *adversarial collaborative* approach. The case is based on IBM's well-known and long-standing relationship with Microsoft. IBM needed a quick-fix solution for its PC business. The company decided to look for a supplier to provide an operating system in the short-term, while it developed its own advanced operating system (OS/2). By misunderstanding the power and opportunity situation in which it was operating, IBM made significant contracting errors and allowed Microsoft to appropriate value that could, and should, have remained with IBM.

The essential problems lay in IBM's assumption that, given its historical dominance in supply innovation in the computer business globally, it could take its time and develop the best in class operating system for the PC. IBM also assumed that the customer would wait for its new system. In short, IBM appears to have believed that when it sourced a quick-fix short-term supply solution externally, it was operating from a position of *buyer dominance*.

Consequently, the company decided not to buy the Microsoft operating system outright. Instead, it adopted an *adversarial arm's-length* approach based on a royalty deal, which equated to Scenario BDOM-1 in Figure 6 in the previous chapter. IBM's decision to adopt this relationship management approach was presumably based on the belief that it would buy relatively few units from Microsoft once its own superior operating system came to market. IBM's operating system was subsequently launched under the name OS/2.

Interestingly, because IBM believed that it was operating from a position of *buyer dominance*, it did not think that it would be necessary to sign an exclusivity deal with Microsoft. Consequently, it allowed the supplier to provide the same operating system to its direct competitors. Unfortunately for IBM, the OS/2 system took so long to come to market that the company ended up competing with quicker to market and lower cost competitors for the same technology. This was Microsoft's operating system, to which IBM did not have ownership rights.

As a result, IBM ended up transferring its initial power advantage in its relationship with Microsoft to the supplier. Over the longer-term, Microsoft was able to use IBM's myopic management decision to create a position of supplier dominance, both in its exchange relationship with IBM and in its relationships with most other PC assemblers.

There seems little doubt that the reason for Microsoft's historical success must owe a great deal to the failure of IBM to understand the objective circumstance within which it was operating in its relationship with Microsoft. IBM believed that it was in a position of *buyer dominance* and used an *adversarial arm's-length* approach to supplier relationship management. The consequence of this was that the company completely lost control of the operating system software, which history has shown to be the most critically valuable asset in the PC. With hindsight, it is clear that when IBM came to source the operating system from Microsoft, the company was actually operating in a position of *interdependence* and should have used an *adversarial collaborative* approach to supplier relationship management.

The reason for this is that when IBM entered into a supply relationship with Microsoft it did not have the capability to produce the operating system software that the market required on its own. In such a circumstance IBM ought to have worked closely with Microsoft, under a tight exclusivity contract, to learn what Microsoft knew so that it could be incorporated into the OS/2 software in the future. By so doing, IBM would have retained complete control over the intellectual property and maximised its appropriation of value from Microsoft's innovation.

While we cannot know with hindsight whether Bill Gates would have accepted such a deal at the time, it seems likely that he would have had to do so. Microsoft could not have achieved the success it has without working with IBM initially. Indeed, it was Microsoft's ability to appropriate ownership and control from IBM over the industrial standard for the PC operating system that was, arguably, the ultimate cause of the company's success. This was granted to Microsoft by IBM's inability to understand the power and opportunity circumstance in which it was operating, and by its inappropriate choice of relationship management strategies.

In effect, IBM started its relationship management approach in Scenario BDOM-1 and tried to maintain that approach. Microsoft, on the other hand, started by choosing to manage this supply relationship in Scenario INT-4. Subsequently, however, Microsoft has been able to manage its relationship with IBM on the basis of a much more beneficial approach from its own perspective, Scenario SDOM-1.

CASE B: THE BUYER OPPORTUNISM CASE

This case explains the problem faced by a company that assumed that it was in a position of *supplier dominance*. The company was using an *adversarial arm's-length* approach to relationship management (Scenario SDOM-1). It did this without realising that its operational practices were placing it at the mercy of a far-sighted buyer. The buyer was ultimately able to achieve a position of dominance combined with *adversarial collaboration* (Scenario BDOM-3).

The case concerns a buying company that decided to outsource its in-house telecommunications systems and equipment to a major supplier. The supplier was the dominant national player in the market place for private and industrial customers. The supplier knew that it was in a dominant situation and that new entrants into the market had considerable barriers to overcome in terms of infrastructure and switching costs. The supplier was also providing services that were operationally critical to the buyer's business. The buyer knew this and accepted that there was no realistic choice other than to go with the incumbent supplier.

This appears to be a classic case of *supplier dominance*, which the supplier was seeking to manage on the basis of an *adversarial arm's-length* relationship (Scenario SDOM-1). The supplier offered the buyer its standard form of contract for a given level of service, against standard fee payments and service level agreements. The supplier believed that the buying company was in a weak position and would be forced to accept the terms of any contract offered.

Unfortunately for the supplier, the buyer in this case was well versed in business strategy and operational implementation. While telecommunications were not core to its business, the buyer recognised that the timely delivery of data was critical to the operational management of its primary supply chains. Furthermore, given the capital investment available, the buyer recognised that it would be unable to keep up with the latest technology if it retained an in-house information system.

The buyer therefore decided to source from an external supplier, which had high technology information systems as its core business, and which was able to keep up with fast-moving international standards of competence in its level of service delivery. Despite the relative strategic dominance of the supplier over the buyer, the buying company understood that there were opportunities for leveraging value for itself from working with a large, cumbersome and bureaucratic company that was complacent.

The buying company understood that, while the supplying company was strategically positioned at Scenario SDOM-1, the operational relationship between the supplier's sales team and the buying company was altogether different. The buyer understood that the sales team operated within a specific business unit that had its own internal targets, and that the sales team was measured on the basis of quarterly sales figures for bonus payments. By offering a close collaborative relationship with the supplier, and by promising to maintain that relationship over a five year period, the buying company used the promise of its long-term dependency in order to extract additional sensitive information from the supplier's sales team.

In so doing, the buyer discovered that the sales team and its business unit needed one major long-term deal, within the next week, in order to become the top sales team that year. The buyer also appreciated that the sales team would individually pocket the consequent bonus payments, but that it was another operational division of the company that would have to deliver the service levels agreed upon in any contract.

The buyer realised, therefore, that a situation of *buyer dominance* could be created operationally, even though the supplier was strategically dominant overall. This was achieved by the use of two tactics. The buyer first threatened to sign a contract with a newly emerging supplier, which had recently been allowed to operate in the national market. Having created uncertainty in the minds of the supplier's sales team, the buyer then offered to cut a deal, but only if it was done immediately and to the buyer's specification. Consequently, because the supplier's sales team was desperate to agree, the standard *adversarial arm's-length* deal (Scenario SDOM-1) offered by the supplier was thrown out.

In this case, the buying company was able to achieve a higher level of service quality at no real cost to itself. Moreover, in return for a long-term contract, the buyer was able to ensure that the service level agreements were set at such a high level that the supplying company was unable to make a profit in the short-term. This was because the supplier constantly had to make penalty payments to the buyer for a failure to meet the agreed service levels.

The buyer achieved significant benefits, and so did the supplier's sales team, but at the expense of the supplying company as a whole. In short, the buyer was able to move the relationship from Scenario SDOM-1 to Scenario INT-3, with considerable short and medium-term benefit to itself. On the other hand, the supplying company experienced an operational loss of its power over the buyer, due to its failure to align its sales and operational delivery teams with the circumstances of power and opportunity in which they found themselves.

CASE C: THE CASE OF THE OVER-MIGHTY BUYER

This is the case of a property management company that had *interdependent, non-adversarial collaborative* relationships with two suppliers (Scenario INT-4). The company mistakenly believed that it could transform these relationships into relationships based on *buyer dominance* combined with *adversarial collaboration* (Scenario BDOM-3). Ultimately, the buying company was forced to abandon its innovative strategy and to return to a position of *interdependence* combined with *non-adversarial collaboration*.

Historically, the property management company in this case had decided that it should not concentrate on the construction of industrial units, but should instead focus on the project appraisal, feasibility and management stages in the development process. This implied the outsourcing of the physical construction and development of the industrial units to suppliers. Even though the supply market for construction companies was highly contested, the buying company decided it would be best to find two preferred suppliers for its construction requirements on a national basis.

The rationale for this approach was based on three main factors. Firstly, the buying company had a regular and predictable spend for this type of work, with plans running many years into the future. Second, the buyer expected that by having two preferred suppliers it would be able to achieve sufficient consolidation of its spend to extract transparency from each of its suppliers in relation to cost and quality issues. Finally, the buying company felt that by limiting the number of suppliers it would reduce its internal transaction costs, as well as provide the basis for a close collaborative working relationship that would encourage mutual innovation in working practices.

The buying company believed that, since the work that it was outsourcing to suppliers was critical to its business, it needed to adopt a *non-adversarial collaborative* approach. Both parties would share in the benefits produced by their collaboration. The buyer would receive transparency and innovation in quality and costs, while the supplier would receive a guarantee of regular work and a share in the benefits gained through innovation and transparency.

The two supplying companies that were eventually selected gave reciprocal support to this approach to relationship management, and were extremely comfortable with it for seven years. After this time, the buying company, due to financial pressure from its parent company, was forced to change the terms of these relationships. The buying company had historically accepted responsibility for 'ground risk'. This is the risk that something unforeseen may occur under the ground that could not reasonably have been foreseen before construction commenced. In such circumstances, the buying company accepted that it, rather than its suppliers, would have to bear any additional costs of construction that might arise.

Due to financial pressure, the buying company decided to move its relationship management approach from *interdependence* combined with *non-adversarial collaboration* (Scenario INT-4) to a *buyer dominance* based, *adversarial collaborative* approach (Scenario BDOM-3). This was achieved by imposing ground risk on the two suppliers. Unfortunately, this approach could not be sustained. After its experience of operating under this regime on two projects, one of the suppliers informed the buying company that it would no longer be able to work on this basis.

The buying company's initial response was to accept this decision and to seek out alternative suppliers from what was, after all, a highly contested supply market with numerous potential suppliers. Interestingly though, while the buying company was able to find a replacement supplier, within six months of awarding this contract it had decided to return to the supplier that it had rejected. On this occasion, however, the relationship was based on cost reimbursable contracts, with the ground risk carried by the buyer. The buying company had been forced to return to its original relationship management approach. It discovered that the operational costs of switching suppliers were so high that it was more cost efficient to source as it had for the previous seven years, rather than to adopt a more aggressive approach.

The reason for this reversal of strategy is fairly easy to understand. A long-term *interdependence* had developed between the buyer and its suppliers over the seven years of working together. As a consequence, the buying company had developed an unrecognised cultural and operational dependency on its suppliers. When the buyer attempted to take advantage of the suppliers by becoming more adversarial in its way of working, it discovered that it could only do so by creating conditions that threatened its own operational performance whenever ground risk was adverse for the supplier.

The buying company believed that it had the potential to move to Scenario BDOM-3, when in reality its only choices were within the scope of *interdependent* relationships, using Scenarios INT-1 through INT-4. Eventually, the company recognised that, to achieve its longer-term operational requirements, it would have to forego short-term financial opportunities by returning to Scenario INT-4.

CASE D: THE MUTUAL BENEFITS OF RECOGNISING INDEPENDENCE

In this case, the mutual benefits that can arise from the recognition by both buyer and supplier of the relative weakness of their respective power positions are explained. The case demonstrates that the buyer had limited business opportunities when it was operating on the basis of *adversarial arm's-length* relationships (Scenario IND-1). When the buyer replaced this relationship management style with a *non-adversarial arm's-length* approach (Scenario IND-2), however, significant mutual benefits were achieved.

The buying company in this case was a nationally based multi-product company. It had an internal organisational structure based on ten autonomous business units, each with its own profit and loss accountabilities to the Group Main Board. All of the business units had a significant and continuous requirement to purchase office stationery for marketing and mail order operations.

Each business unit had its own purchasing division, with an independent approach to purchasing. Two of the business units had no effective procurement strategy, and were awarding contracts to the same supplier simply on the basis of historical attachment. The eight remaining business units acquired their supplies by aggressively market testing in what was, and still is, a highly contested market place characterised by many suppliers and relatively low switching costs for buyers. As a result, the buying company had a continually changing supply base, with no consolidation of spend and often up to nine different suppliers for the same item at any one time.

Interestingly enough, not only did the buying company fragment its spend, but it also incurred extremely high internal transaction costs in eight of its business units through the use of annual market testing of suppliers. The buying company had not recognised that there are significant internal costs associated with organising competitions, that are part of the total costs of ownership for any buyer. Ironically, even when buying the company did not incur these internal transaction costs, through the buying inertia of two of its business units, this benefit was inadvertent and more than offset by incompetence elsewhere. The most significant problem was that the prices being paid by these two complacent business units were almost double those being achieved by the best of the business units that were testing the market on a regular basis.

Despite the success achieved by some of the business units, however, it was clear that the buying company's autonomous procurement structure was significantly limiting the cost and quality improvement opportunities available to the company as a whole in this area of spend. The problem was that the ten business units significantly fragmented the total spend for office stationary that the company could bring to the market, and thereby reduced its potential leverage with any individual supplier. More importantly, the *adversarial arm's-length* approach used by a majority of the business units undermined the ability of any potential supplier to offer a better deal on price or quality for the total spend that the company was sourcing annually.

This problem was further compounded by the fact that the buying company's relative power and opportunity position in the market place would not be significantly augmented even if it decided (as it eventually did) to consolidate its expenditure on stationery. Even with its total spend consolidated, the buying company's requirements were a very small percentage of the total national market for office stationery (less than 0.01%). This situation implied that the leverage position of the buyer was not likely to improve significantly if the company maintained an *adversarial arm's-length* approach to suppliers.

Given the relative weakness of the buyer's power and opportunity position, it was apparent that the company would have to adopt a very different approach if it wanted to improve the current cost and quality performance. The buying company therefore decided to seek out, after an initial market testing exercise, a single source supplier for all of its office stationery requirements. This single source deal was awarded on the understanding that the supplier's cost and quality performance would be continuously monitored against that of other suppliers. If the supplier were able to match the best in class performance, then it would retain the contract.

The buying company justified this approach on the basis that the market was highly contested, with many suppliers offering interchangeable products with relatively low switching costs. Consequently, the buyer faced a low level of commercial risk by awarding a consolidated long-term contract to a single preferred supplier.

By doing so, the buying company was able to achieve a significant reduction in the initial cost of purchase. This was achieved through buying higher volumes and from the certainty that the supplier received by being awarded a long-term contract. The buyer was also able to achieve a secondary cost reduction by ending a wasteful duplication of internal staff resource and effort. Overall then, the buying company was able to record a significant reduction in the total cost of ownership. It also achieved a higher level of supplier responsiveness to the specific needs of each of the ten business units.

The buying company achieved these benefits, because it was able to recognise that, while it was in a position of *independence vis-à-vis* the supplier, a *non-adversarial arm's-length* approach with a preferred supplier would reduce the total costs of ownership. The benefits were not, however, all one sided. The supplier recognised that by cutting its prices, and by working continuously to provide a better customer response, it would lose some of the profit margin that it might have achieved had it priced opportunistically.

Nonetheless, the supplier also recognised that it would have the compensatory benefit of a larger and more certain volume of business from the buyer. The supplier realised that it ought to thereby be able to achieve economies of scale in its production operations, and have the opportunity to obtain greater market share and competitive strength. The supplier also recognised that it would be able to use the fact that it was supplying a major nationally known company as part of its marketing strategy with other potential customers.

This case should not be taken to mean, however, that a *non-adversarial arm's-length* approach is always the most appropriate way of managing an exchange relationship under circumstances of buyer-supplier independence. It simply means that in the circumstances of *independence* in this particular case, a *non-adversarial arm's-length* approach (Scenario IND-2) was much more beneficial for both parties than the *adversarial arm's-length* approach that they had historically adopted.

CHAPTER VII

RE-ENGINEERING THE DNA OF BUSINESS AND SUPPLY CHAIN LIFE

One of the great tragedies of our lives is that we have to learn to work within the limits that our biology imposes on us. If there is something physical that we do not like about ourselves, generally speaking, we have to put up with it. If we are overweight, for example, the option to diet does exist, but our tendency to add pounds is not something that will just go away. And, of course, three months working out in a gym will not make our feet one size smaller or our chin one inch less pronounced, however much we may desire such changes. We are pretty much stuck with the hand that has been dealt us. Successive generations, of course, may fare better than ours. But the pace of this change is a slow process and, although we may take comfort from the fact that our children represent a biological improvement, that doesn't help our own personal situation.

This lack of biological flexibility is no small thing and its effects can be catastrophic. Some time around 60 million years ago, a giant asteroid collided with the Earth, wiping out a class of animals that had survived and dominated the planet for millions of years. In the face of such an event, any organism would have been hard pushed to survive. In fact, there have been five such events recorded in biological history and the biggest of these (which ended the Permian Period, 250 million years ago) wiped out nearly all life on Earth. The dinosaurs, however, were particularly ill suited to weather the cosmological storm.

There are rules to extinction and the rules would seem to be these. First, there is a size bias. Big animals tend to disappear more readily than small animals. Second, small populations tend to be more vulnerable than large ones. There are fewer animals for the giant rock to kill. Finally, geographical spread is also a factor. If everything dies in Europe and North America but there are pockets of survivors in Australasia, then a species has a chance of bouncing back. Dinosaurs, however, were unlucky on all three counts. They were obviously big animals and even before the asteroid struck they were a species in decline. Furthermore, where once they had roamed the globe, by 60 million years BC they were increasingly confined to the North American continent.

Supply chain management is, as we have seen, at least in part concerned with the subject of commercial ecology: the environment in which firms operate and the resources and competencies that they bring to that environment. However, commercial ecology, unlike biological ecology, is not Darwinian. In Darwinian ecology, an organism's DNA is fixed – although genetic engineering is changing this – so that if it is not suited to the environment in which it operates, its maladaptation causes it to die. Commercial ecology, by contrast, is Lamarkian. Lamarkian evolution offers the firm repeated bites of the cherry. If a software house needs to update its products in order to compete, it can attempt to update them. If an entrepreneur sees a market opportunity then it can be pursued. When either event happens, of course, it is impacting directly on a firm's power resources and, thus, the dynamics of supply chain exchange.

In the preceding chapter, we considered the issue of relationship styles and their appropriateness to particular power structures. When undertaking supply chain management all firms have to be concerned with such issues. However, as a strategy it is largely reactive in that it is responding to *what is*. It is effectively the same as asking how do I best play the hand that I have been dealt? It is Charles Darwin's lion, fox, pigeon or grasshopper, building its approach to survival around the biology it has inherited. An alternative approach, however, is to return to the deck and to centre one's strategy on changing one's biology. This approach is about Lamarkian ecology and supply chain re-engineering.

This concept of supply chain re-engineering requires the firm to think about two distinct sets of issues. First, it requires the firm to have a clear idea about where it wants to go. That is, it must have a clear conception of the supply chain structures that it wishes to create.

In chapter four we suggested that all supply chains are idiosyncratic and that these idiosyncrasies impact directly upon the flow of value through the chain. We also contended that some structures worked better for the firm than others. We implied, although we did not develop the contention, that what benefited the firm most was supply chain dominance. That is, a series of interlocking relationships that placed the firm in a dominant position at the heart of the structure. In a supply chain that approximates to the following hypothetical example, A < B < C > D > E > F, firm C would be ideally placed to undertake the task of supply chain co-ordination. Its dominance would be *Janus-faced* in that it would run both upstream over its suppliers and downstream over its customers. Thereafter, firm would be free to choose how to manage the chain. It might opt for a collaborative approach to supply chain management, confident that if it needed to crack the whip it could do so.

Conversely, firm C could pursue (as arguably Japanese carmakers have done) a policy of *adversarial collaboration*. We have argued elsewhere that this is potentially an immensely powerful strategy. Describing it as *one-eyed* lean supply, we have made the claim that it simultaneously offers the firm the efficiency gains of collaboration without the need to share them amongst all of the participants of the network.

The second set of issues that confronts the firm attempting a re-engineering strategy is how does it get there? The answer to this question lies in developing a fuller understanding of supply chain DNA or the resources that can confer power upon the firm.

Wanting to be powerful and becoming powerful are two completely different things. For example, trying as drug companies do to create market power through non-replicable innovation actually requires the company to develop something that has demonstrable clinical value. Attempting, as some supermarkets do to obtain an advantage through the convenience of their locations presupposes that the sites on which they hope to build are available. If an organisation's re-engineering strategy is not simply to degenerate into a wish list, it must possess the internal capabilities that will allow it to align intent with achievement.

Furthermore, the firm should also recognise the fact that although all power resources will assist it in its attempts to appropriate value, not all resources are equally effective, sustainable or commercially cost-effective. A few examples will serve to illustrate the point.

The difficulty for firms seeking downstream dominance through innovation is that this innovation is frequently highly speculative, costly and the advantage that it confers is short lived. One of the phenomena of the 1980s and 1990s has been the emergence of computer game technology. Leading the way in the attempt to colonise children's bedrooms have been companies like Nintendo, Sega, Atari and Sony. What instantly stands out about this list is that Atari is no longer a major player and that Nintendo and Sega are also struggling to keep their places in the market.

The fall of Nintendo has been particularly dramatic. The company spent millions of dollars developing the N64 only to find that when it was finally launched, consumers were already happy with the Sony technology that was in place. This was money down the drain. The only people possibly to benefit from it were the employees and suppliers who had helped to develop the product.

Other mechanisms of market closure are problematic in that, while they are undoubtedly effective, they also invite the attention of the competition authorities. Microsoft, for example, owes its dominance to its ownership of an industry-standard PC operating system in which its customers have a high sunk cost. It attempts to replicate this position with its Internet browser have invited one of the most public anti-trust suits since the beginning of the last century.

In direct contrast to the above, commercial advantages based upon some types of information asymmetry have proven to be both cheap to develop and virtually regulation-proof. Everybody who has ever bought a house or tried to process a will knows that lawyers do not come cheap. They are also probably aware that the levels of legal training to undertake these simple tasks are probably not very high. Despite these twin facts most people still hire lawyers rather than undertake the work themselves. This is because the difficulties and costs associated with developing even relatively low levels of legal expertise are regarded as prohibitive.

So, notwithstanding the numbers of lawyers practising in this day and age, price competition between them is at best limited. Furthermore, a lawyer is not even required to be particularly competent at what they do. What they offer is a credence good and the point about such goods is that their quality cannot be judged even after consumption. Your lawyer may have lost you thousands of dollars (and charged you thousands for the privilege as well), but who can say that his or her competitor down the road would have done any better.

So, where do all of these insights leave the reader? We hope that they leave them with a better understanding of supply chains than they started out with. We hope, for example, that they have a clearer view of the role of collaboration in supply chain management. We hope, too, that they have a clearer idea of what collaboration itself means. One thing that the reader should have been left with is a clear understanding that 'partnership' is not the only form of collaboration and that it should never be regarded as an end in itself. At most, it is merely a means to an end and one whose success is likely to be shaped by the context in which it is employed.

Finally, it is hoped that the reader will be left with the realisation that there is still a great deal that they still do not know about the subject of supply chains. They are not alone. Plato once observed that to expand one's knowledge is also to enlarge one's ignorance. When we are children our understanding of the world is limited to those things that we directly encounter – at the time, of course, we do not realise just how much this is the case. Before we study mathematics for the first time we probably have no idea that such a thing even exists. Once we discover that it does, however, we start to recognise that our understanding of the world is more partial than we previously thought.

Whilst undertaking the research for this book, and for its companion volume, we became aware that there is a great deal that people do not understand about supply chains and the *power regimes* that exist within them. This is why the EPSRC was prepared to advance us the money to do the research in the first place. Now that we have got to this point, we can confidently claim that we understand supply chains much better than we did before we started out.

We also recognise, however, that there is still a great deal about supply chains that we do not understand and that the subject is much more complex than we could ever have imagined. This must be frustrating for the practitioner who both needs and desires workable answers – now. For the academic, however, this is precisely what makes his or her life so challenging and rewarding.

FURTHER READING

Bleeke, J. and D. Ernst (1996), *Collaborating to Compete: Using Strategic Alliances and Acquisitions in the Global Marketplace* (New York: John Wiley & Sons).

Brandenburger, A. M. and B. J. Nalebuff (1996), *Co-opetition* (New York: Doubleday).

Christopher, M. (1992), *Logistics and Supply Chain Management* (London: Pitman).

Christopher, M. (1997), *Marketing Logistics* (Oxford: Butterworth Heinemann).

Connolly, W. E. (1974), *The Terms of Political Discourse* (Oxford: Basil Blackwell).

Cook, K. (1977), 'Exchange and power in networks of inter-organizational relations', *Sociological Quarterly*, Vol. 18, pp. 62-82.

Cook, K., R. Emerson, M. Gillmore and T. Yamagishi (1983), 'The distribution of power in exchange networks', *American Journal of Sociology*, Vol. 89, pp. 275-305.

Cox, A. (1997), *Business Success: A Way of Thinking about Strategy, Critical Supply Chain Assets and Operational Best Practice* (Boston, UK: Earlsgate Press, www. earlsgatepress.com).

Cox, A. (1997), 'On power, appropriateness and procurement competence', *Supply Management*, 2nd October, pp. 24-27.

Cox, A. (1999), 'Power, value and supply chain management', *Supply Chain Management*, Vol. 4, No. 4, pp. 167-175.

Cox, A. (1999), 'Improving procurement and supply competence: on the appropriate use of reactive and proactive tools and techniques in the public and private sectors', in Lamming, R. and A. Cox (eds), *Strategic Procurement Management: Concepts and Cases* (Boston, UK: Earlsgate Press, www.earlsgatepress.com).

Cox, A. (2000), *Effective Supply Chain Management* (Boston, UK: Earlsgate Press, www.earlsgatepress.com).

Cox, A., P. Ireland, C. Lonsdale, J. Sanderson and G. Watson (2000), *Supply Chains, Markets and Power: Mapping Buyer and Supplier Power Regimes* (Forthcoming).

Cox A. and G. Watson (2000), 'On power and efficiency: rediscovering the ghost in the machine of the economic institutions of capitalism', *CBSP Working Paper 1/2000* (Birmingham: Centre for Business Strategy and Procurement, Birmingham Business School).

Emerson, R. E. (1962), 'Power-dependence relations', *American Sociological Review*, Vol. 27, pp. 31-41.

Gallie, W.B. (1955/6), 'Essentially contested concepts', *Proceedings of the Aristotelian Society*, Vol.56, pp. 170-171.

Gattorna, J. L. and D. W. Walters (1996), *Managing the Supply Chain* (Basingstoke: Macmillan).

Harrison, A. (1993), *Just-in-Time Manufacturing in Perspective* (London: Prentice Hall).

Hines, P. (1994), *Creating World Class Suppliers* (London: Pitman).

Hines, P. et al. (2000), *Value Stream Management* (Harlow: Prentice Hall).

Jenkins, M. (1998), *Genetics* (London: Hodder Headline).

Kapoor, V. and A. Gupta (1997), 'Aggressive Sourcing: A free market approach', *Sloan Management Review*, Fall, pp. 21-31.

Lacity, M. and L. Willcocks (1996), *Best Practices in Information Technology Sourcing* (Oxford, The Oxford Executive Research Briefings).

Lamming, R. (1993), *Beyond Partnership* (New York: Prentice Hall).

Laseter, T. M. (1998), *Balanced Sourcing: Co-operation and Competition in Supplier Relationships* (San Francisco: Jossey-Bass Publishers).

Lonsdale, C. and A. Cox (1998), *Outsourcing: A Business Guide to Risk Management Tools and Techniques* (Boston, UK: Earlsgate Press, www.earlsgatepress.com).

Lukes, S. (1974), *Power: A Radical View* (London: Macmillan).

Molho, I. (1997), *The Economics of Information: Lying and Cheating in Markets and Organisations* (Oxford: Blackwell Publishers Ltd).

Moore, J. F. (1996), *The Death of Competition* (New York: Harper Collins).

Pfeffer, J. and G. R. Salancik (1978), *The External Control of Organizations: A Resource Dependence Perspective* (New York: Harper & Row).

Porter, M. E. (1980), *Competitive Strategy: Techniques for Analysing Industries and Competitors* (New York: The Free Press).

Porter, M. E. (1996), 'What is Strategy?' *Harvard Business Review*, November-December, pp. 61-78.

Raup, D. (1993), *Extinction – Bad Genes or Bad Luck?* (Oxford, Oxford University Press).

Rumelt, R. P. (1984), 'Towards a strategic theory of the firm', in R. Lamb (ed.), *Competitive Strategic Management* (Englewood Cliffs, NJ: Prentice Hall).

Rumelt, R. P. (1987), 'Theory, strategy and entrepreneurship', in D. Teece (ed.), *The Competitive Challenge* (New York: Harper & Row).

Saunders, M. (1994), *Strategic Purchasing and Supply Chain Management* (London: Pitman).

Scott, C. and R. Westbrook (1991), 'New strategic tools for supply chain management', *International Journal of Physical Distribution and Logistics Management*, Vol. 21, No. 1, pp. 23-33.

Watson, G. and J. Sanderson (1997) 'Collective goods versus private interest: Lean enterprise and the free rider problem', in A. Cox and P. Hines (eds.), *Advanced Supply Management: The Best Practice Debate* (Boston, UK: Earlsgate Press, www.earlsgatepress.com).

Willcocks, L.P. and M. C. Lacity (eds) (1998), *Strategic Sourcing of Information Systems: Perspectives and Practices* (Chichester: John Wiley).

Williamson, O. E. (1985), *The Economic Institutions of Capitalism* (New York: The Free Press).

Womack, J. P. and D. T. Jones (1994), 'From lean production to lean enterprise' *Harvard Business Review*, Vol. 64, pp. 34-47.

Womack, J. P. and D. T. Jones (1996), *Lean Thinking: Banish Waste and Create Wealth in your Organisation* (New York: Simon Schuster).

Womack, J. P., D. T. Jones and D. Roos (1990), *The Machine that Changed the World* (New York: Rawson Associates).

Yoshino, M. Y. and U. S. Rangan (1995), *Strategic Alliances: An Entrepreneurial Approach to Globalisation* (Boston, MA: Harvard Business School Press).